STARTING SEEDS

How to Grow Healthy, Productive Vegetables, Herbs, and Flowers from Seed

Barbara W. Ellis

Storey Publishing

*The mission of Storey Publishing is to serve our customers by
publishing practical information that encourages
personal independence in harmony with the environment.*

Edited by Carleen Madigan
Art direction by Jessica Armstrong
Text production by Theresa Wiscovitch

Cover illustration by © Meg Hunt
Interior illustrations by © Kagan McLeod

Indexed by Christine R. Lindemer, Boston Road Communications

Storey Publishing
210 MASS MoCA Way
North Adams, MA 01247
www.storey.com

Printed in the United States by McNaughton & Gunn, Inc.
10   9   8   7   6   5   4   3   2   1

Library of Congress Cataloging-in-Publication Data

Ellis, Barbara W.   631.53
  Starting seeds / by Barbara Ellis.
    p. cm.
  Includes index.
  ISBN 978-1-61212-105-5 (pbk. : alk. paper)
  ISBN 978-1-60342-850-7 (e-book)
  1. Plant propagation. 2. Seeds. 3. Sowing. I. Title.
SB119.E45 2013
631.5'3—dc23
                    2012032602

CONTENTS

THE MAGIC OF SEEDS

Seed packets begin arriving at my house every year in midwinter. I gather them like trading cards: a couple from one source, a few from another. In addition to purchased packets, my annual collection also includes bundles of treasures from seed exchanges and envelopes from friends and fellow gardeners. When it comes time to turn them all into a garden, my bundle becomes more like a deck of playing cards, rather than the trading type. Timing and the rules of the game play major roles in transforming a batch of seed packets into a thriving garden.

It's important to remember that the seeds basically set the rules. The secret to starting them successfully is understanding what they need to grow. Successful gardeners aren't playing a game of 52 Pickup, though, where cards are flung in the air to land randomly and be picked up as quickly as possible. Instead, think games like bridge or canasta, where patience, system, and strategy are key.

Fortunately, seed sowing is easy to learn. Success is simple once you understand a few basic principles, such as what seeds need to sprout and how to schedule sowing so plants are ready to go into the garden once the weather — and you — are ready for them.

Seed Starting Basics provides all the information you need to turn a pile of seed packets into a successful garden. In it, you'll learn easy ways to sow seeds and manage seedlings, indoors and out; how to select pots and potting mix; and how to develop a seed-sowing schedule that works for you and for your garden. This book also explains how to raise sturdy, healthy seedlings and get them off and growing in the garden.

WHY SEEDS?

BUYING PLANTS AT THE LOCAL GARDEN CENTER or big box store may be quick and easy, but these outlets only have room to offer a limited selection of plants. Starting from seeds lets you choose from the incredibly diverse selection of vegetables and flowers that are not readily available as plants. You can choose the best high-yielding hybrids, or unusual heirlooms your grandmother grew, or plants that will withstand your particular climate. There's little doubt growing your own plants from seed will give you a sense of pride and accomplishment. Here are a few other reasons why starting plants from seeds makes sense:

1. **Save money!** Growing plants from seeds is less expensive than buying the plants. That's true even if you purchase basic tools and equipment highlighted in this book. If you already have the equipment, seeds are a lot less expensive than plants.

2. **Go organic.** If safe, chemical-free food is one reason you garden, controlling your food from seed to table just makes sense.

3. **Experiment.** Try the best new releases, a different transplant time, or plant a few vegetables you've never grown before — all without spending much money.

4. **Set your own schedule.** Garden centers and other outlets offer plants when "most" people are planting. To try a new schedule, plant extra early for a bigger harvest, or grow crops in tunnels over the winter, you'll need to start your own from seeds.

5. **Sow where they're to grow.** Some vegetables and flowers simply resent being transplanted (see page 42). You'll get the best results if you sow these in the garden right where

the plants are to grow. Or, sow in biodegradable containers, so that seedlings can be transplanted pot and all! (See page 40 for more on this option.)

6. **Grow a gardener.** By teaching a child how to sow seeds, you can grow gardeners as you plant. Children love fast-germinating seeds like bush beans, marigolds, zinnias, sunflowers, or morning glories.

7. **Start slowly.** If you're a new gardener, start with just a few packets — ideally a mix of some that can be sown outdoors where the plants are to grow, and a couple for indoor sowing. See Start with the Easy Ones on page 7 for more ideas.

PART 1

GETTING STARTED

Many kinds of seeds sprout quickly and reliably without anything more than even moisture and light. This is especially true of annuals, but perennials, trees, shrubs, and vines can all be started from seed as well — they just require a little extra patience. While seed-sowing takes some strategy and attention to detail, and specific germination requirements vary from plant to plant, the good news is that the basics are pretty much the same for all types of seeds.

In this section, you'll find information on everything from choosing plants to buying seeds and using the information on seed packets. You'll learn how to figure out how many seeds to buy, how to test whether seeds are too old (if you've held onto them from previous seasons), and how to harvest and save your own seeds. You'll see how to develop a sowing and planting schedule that is adapted for your garden. In addition, you'll find information on common problems and how to deal with them.

WHAT DO YOU WANT TO GROW?

TWIRLING SEED RACKS AT A LOCAL GARDEN CENTER — or pondering choices in catalogs or on websites — is a fun way to get into seed starting. The gorgeous pictures on packets, coupled with the promise of new life inside, can be extremely seductive. Every possibility seems more attractive than the last. Even though packets only cost a few dollars each, it's easy to quickly run up a tab. It simply makes sense to set parameters about what you want to grow before you stock up.

One step that greatly increases your chances of success is to take a hard look at your yard to see the exposure and other conditions plants growing there will be facing. Use this information to make a list of plants that grow best in the conditions naturally found in your yard — sun, shade; poor soil or rich, for example. To identify possibilities, use the lists in this book, ask gardening friends, and search the Internet. Starting with a list of suitable plants greatly improves your chances of success, because you only have to help plants along, not fight the site at the same time. See Get to Know Your Garden on page 10 for tips on what to look for when evaluating your site. Here are some other considerations to help focus your choices.

Pick the Crops You Really Want

It's important to be more specific than "nice vegetables" or "pretty flowers" here. Start by asking yourself what vegetables you really like to eat. If you have kids, what do they like to eat? Filling your garden with food you love, rather than crops you think you should grow, just makes sense. Why work hard to grow something that no one in the family is really excited about eating? Once you've identified a few crops to try, consider looking past the obvious choices. Experiment with purple peppers or yellow, star-shaped summer squash. They aren't any harder to grow than the ordinary kinds you find on every farm stand in summer. Another option is to concentrate on vegetables that are expensive or that you can never get enough of — grape tomatoes and sugar snap peas, for example.

If you want to grow flowers, narrow your choices in much the same way. Perhaps flowers for cut or dried bouquets top your list, or blooms that are fragrant or attract butterflies to the garden. Some seed catalogs and websites offer popular annuals packaged by color, so you can plant all pink or yellow zinnias, for example, to ensure that blooms blend with other plants in your garden.

Start with the Easy Ones

If you've never sown seeds before, or if previous attempts didn't turn out well, embrace your beginner status. Concentrate on easy-to-grow crops for both indoor starting and out. Sticking with just a few selections also makes learning easier and increases success. Fill in with purchased plants, and add more plants from seed as you gain experience.

Fast and cool. Fast-growing, cool-weather crops are among the easiest ones to grow. The following can be sown right in the garden where they are to grow. Plant small batches of seeds in spring and more batches in late summer to harvest in fall.

- Arugula
- Beets
- Leaf lettuce
- Mesclun
- Radishes
- Snap or bush peas
- Spinach

Crops for summer. Many of the heat-loving summer crops that are easy to grow take a bit longer than the cool-season crops above. Best bets include:

- Bush-type green beans
- Bush-type squash and zucchini
- Peppers
- Swiss chard
- Tomatoes

Herbs from seed. Parsley, dill, chervil, and cilantro (coriander) are all easy herbs that can be sown in spring, out in the garden where the plants are to grow. Basil, which prefers warm temperatures, can also be sown outdoors but is often started indoors to give plants a head start. Parsley plants can also benefit from a head start indoors, but they resent being transplanted, so sow them in paper or peat pots. (See Pots for Fussy Seedlings on page 42.) Many perennial herbs are best propagated by division or cuttings because they don't come true from seed, meaning seedlings may not resemble their parent plant. Chives are probably the easiest perennial herbs to grow from seed, but thyme, sage, and lavender can also be started this way.

Fresh Is Best

Start each season with fresh seed packaged for the current year. Leftover seed may be inexpensive, and half-empty packets from a friend may be free, but unless stored properly the seeds may no longer be capable of germinating. If you do start with seed saved from a previous season, make sure it was stored properly (cool and dry), and do a germination test before gambling on it. See Any Life Left? on page 22 for more information.

....

Vegetables for Shade

Even if you don't have an ideal, 8-hour, full-sun site for vegetables, don't despair. The crops below all grow just fine with a half day of sun. Ones marked with a + will grow in full shade, but they grow best when they receive good light, so pick the brightest spot you have available.

- Arugula+
- Beans (bush types are best)
- Beets
- Bok choi/pak choi
- Broccoli
- Carrots
- Collards
- Endive+
- Kale
- Lettuce, head and leaf+
- Mesclun+
- Mustard
- Peas (bush types are best)
- Potatoes
- Radicchio+
- Radishes
- Scallions
- Spinach
- Swiss chard+
- Turnips

....

GET TO KNOW YOUR GARDEN

EVEN BEFORE YOU SOW THAT FIRST SEED — or order that first seed packet — it pays to learn about the growing conditions your yard has to offer. Once you know how much sun a gardening site receives, or the type of soil a bed contains, selecting seeds becomes easier, because you can choose plants that will thrive in the conditions there. That not only improves plant performance and your success rate, it also reduces maintenance since it is easier to provide seedlings with the conditions they need to thrive.

SITE SELECTION. When looking for an ideal garden spot, consider the amount of sun each site receives. Raised beds are useful for improving soil on poor sites, and a spot protected from prevailing wind is also beneficial for plants.

To grow most vegetables successfully, be prepared to consider various sites to maximize sun exposure. You also may need to make a plan to improve the soil to accommodate the plants you want to grow. If you don't have great sites — or a space for growing plants in the ground at all — the good news is that many vegetables and flowers thrive in containers. Here are some things to look for:

How much sun and shade? Observe your yard several times throughout a day. Make notes about how much sun or shade different sites receive. Vegetables and many annual flowers need spots that receive full sun — at least 8 hours per day. Full-shade plants don't need any direct sun, but they do need good indirect light, so the deep shade found under dense evergreens isn't suitable. Plants that take partial shade generally need at least 4 hours of direct sun, so a site that faces east or west may work. Sites with sun filtered through overhanging deciduous trees suit a great many shade-loving plants.

Learn about the soil. Test the soil to determine its pH. Also determine the soil type, which affects sowing times. Clay soil stays wet and cold longer in spring than sandy soil does, for example. For information on testing soil, contact your local Cooperative Extension office. Asking nearby friends and neighbors can also help determine the kind of soil you are dealing with.

Study extremes. Identify spots that are especially windy or exposed to late afternoon heat and sun, as well as sites that stay wet in spring or where puddles linger for a long time after a rain. Once you understand the extreme conditions that exist, you can avoid them (as by siting your garden in a spot protected from prevailing winds), or picking plants that can withstand them.

SEED SAVVY

GOOD-QUALITY CATALOGS, websites, and seed packets offer a wealth of information. Companies want their seeds to grow successfully in your garden, so they provide as much growing information as possible. Photographs and tempting descriptions are hard to miss, but here are some of the other information and terms you will encounter.

Catalog Information

Companies have limited space on seed packets, so the amount of information they contain is limited. Read packets, but also look at catalogs and website listings for the following information about seeds you buy.

Packet size or seeds per ounce. Use this information to determine how many seeds you are buying. Some catalogs offer several different size packets so gardeners with different size gardens can buy the quantity they need. Though price per seed is cheaper with larger packets, resist the temptation to buy large amounts that will last you several years. You're better off starting with fresh seed.

Germination time, temperature, and timing. You should at least find the number of days from sowing to sprouting and a recommended temperature. Many companies also provide plant spacing and growing guidelines, crop timing suggestions, harvest suggestions, and other information. This information may be listed under the general entry for the vegetable or flower, such as pumpkins or sunflowers, rather than with the descriptions of the individual cultivars — 'Orange Smoothie' pumpkin or 'Valentine' sunflower, for example — and varies from company to company.

Days to maturity. This is the number of days for the plant to reach harvest size or begin flowering, but it is calculated two different ways depending on the crop. For crops that are typically sown right in the garden where they are to grow — carrots and peas, for example — "days to maturity" means days from sowing to first harvest. For crops that are typically started indoors and transplanted, such as peppers and cabbage, days to maturity is from the transplant date. Read carefully to determine which way days to maturity is being calculated for each crop you're considering.

SEED SHAPES AND SIZES. Seeds come in all shapes and sizes, from dustlike petunia seed to giants like lima beans.

Seed Types and Terms

These are common terms that you'll find in plant descriptions. Understanding them will help you choose which seeds to buy. You'll find more terms under Easy Flowers Outdoors on page 110.

Heirloom. This term is generally used to describe cultivated varieties of plants that originated before the 1940s, although it is also used to describe selections that are more than 40 years old. Seeds from heirlooms can be collected and saved for future gardens. See Saving and Storing Secrets on page 32 for more information.

Hybrid. A plant that is the result of cross-pollination between two distinct parent plants. Hybrids can be naturally occurring, as when a bee pollinates two different plants, or when plant breeders purposely cross two plants. *F1* hybrids* are created by crossing parent plants from two distinct lines. *F2* hybrids* are created by crossing plants from two F1* hybrid lines. Since seed from hybrids may or may not produce plants that resemble the hybrid itself, there's no sense collecting and saving seed from these plants for future gardens. To grow them again, you have to buy new hybrid seed, since the parent lines must be re-crossed each time to produce hybrid seed for the next generation.

Open-pollinated. Plants that are freely pollinated by bees, wind, or other method without intervention by gardeners. Open-pollinated (OP) plants, including heirloom vegetables, are perpetuated by gardeners collecting, saving, and replanting the seed.

Organic. The term "certified organic" has a distinct legal meaning in a catalog or on a seed packet. It indicates that the seed was produced by a grower who has complied with all the rules specified by the U.S. Department of Agriculture's National Organic Program. That means the seed was produced on land that has not been exposed to synthetic fertilizers or pesticides for 3 years. The regulation also prohibits use of sewage sludge, irradiation, and genetic engineering.

Treated/untreated. Although normally only sold to farmers for large-scale operations, treated seed is coated with a fungicide to help prevent it from rotting in cold or wet soil. Some companies who sell packets of seed to homeowners offer treated seed. It is not currently an accepted treatment for certified organic seed, although acceptable organic treatments may become available.

Pelleted Seed

Seeds that are pelleted are covered with inert materials such as clay and starches to make them easier to handle. Companies typically offer pelleted seed for vegetables and flowers that have especially tiny seeds (carrots and petunias, for example). Pelleted seed is more expensive than unpelleted seed, but the process makes it easier to sow seeds evenly, which reduces the need to thin seedlings later on. It also makes it easier to spread seeds using mechanized seeders.

HOW MANY PACKETS?

"HOW MANY PLANTS DO I NEED?" is what you really need to ask. It pays to do a quick bit of calculating before ordering and again before sowing. Otherwise, it's easy to end up with twice as many tomatoes or marigolds as you have room for in the garden. Keep in mind you'll likely want more than one cultivar of some plants — lettuce, beans, and zinnias, for example — so you'll need several different packets of your choices. Here are tips to keep you on track:

Don't just guesstimate. For a more accurate idea of what you need, measure the garden space available, then use the recommendations on the seed packet to determine about how many plants will fill it. For example, a row that's 10 feet long and 1 foot wide accommodates 12 plants spaced on 10-inch centers. (See Spacing: Beds, Rows, or Broadcasting? on page 99 for a more efficient way to fit more plants in a smaller area.) Plant a few more seeds than you need — say, 20 percent extra — for insurance against losses.

You don't have to sow it all. Seed of fast-growing crops like lettuce, mesclun, and radishes also can be planted a little at a time. That way, you can produce several small crops over a long season, rather than one huge crop. See Cycle Your Sowing on page 29.

Consider purchasing plants for some crops. Tomatoes are large and bear over a long season, so you may only have room for four or five of them. In that case, plants may be a better option, especially since you may want to grow several *different* tomatoes. The same goes for summer squash or zucchini. One plant per squash eater in the household is generally plenty. If limited indoor growing space is an issue, it may make sense to buy seedlings for crops such as tomatoes, peppers, and eggplant that need to be started indoors because they take so long to reach maturity.

Keeping Track

Whether you're sowing indoors or out, keeping track of which crops are planted where is essential. In addition to a notebook and/or calendar for making note of sowing and transplant dates, labels are key. Without them, every soil-filled container soil looks the same, and it's far too easy to forget just where the lettuce or love-in-a-mist seed was scattered outdoors. Use small 3- or 4-inch labels for indoor sowing, and larger — 12 inches or so — for outdoor sowings. Plastic or wooden labels are fine. Buy them with your seed order, or cut labels from recycled plastic cups (like the ones yogurt is sold in). Use plastic for perennials, since the labels are longer lasting. For writing on labels, an ordinary pencil is ideal. Not only is the writing durable — it lasts much longer than ballpoint pen or a permanent marker — you can also erase it to recycle the label. Or buy a nursery marking pen. Waterproof and resistant to fading by the sun, they're handy for writing on everything from labels or wooden markers to pots.

DO-IT-YOURSELF SEED TAPES

Available from many seed companies, seed tapes make spacing seeds a simple task. To plant, just lay the strip on the ground, cover lightly with soil (see the seed packet for optimum depth), water, and wait! Seed tapes are an expensive way to buy seeds, though, plus choices are limited. Fortunately, they're easy to assemble. Making them is a great winter project. Seed tapes are especially handy for giving tiny seed like lettuce or carrots the correct spacing, but they can be made from any kind of seeds. They also make great gifts for friends and beginning gardeners. Here's how:

1. Mix flour with enough water to make a soupy paste a little thicker than the consistency of ketchup.

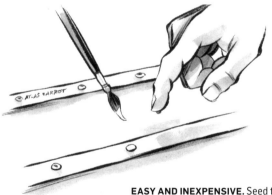

EASY AND INEXPENSIVE. Seed tapes make spacing a snap at planting time. By making them yourself, you get to pick the crops you want to grow. They're a great, easy-to-make winter project, and inexpensive, too!

2. Cut black-and-white newspaper or paper towels into 1-inch-wide strips. Any length is fine.

3. With the paint brush, dab flour paste onto a paper strip, then press a seed into place. Space dabs and seeds according to the spacing directions on the seed packet.

4. Write the name of the seed on each strip, and leave the strips spread out until the flour paste dries.

5. Fold or roll up the dry strips and store in a plastic container or bag until planting time.

Keep It Local

Regional seed companies are a great source. Not only do they offer seed of plants that perform well in local climate conditions — summertime heat and humidity in the Southeast, or short growing seasons in the North or mountainous regions — they also often have valuable local information about scheduling on their websites or in their catalogs.

GERMINATION 101

SEEDS ARE AMAZING STRUCTURES, whether they are large, like beans or corn kernels, or tiny and dustlike, like the seeds of petunias or begonias. Each seed contains a tiny plant embryo complete with a root, shoot, and an initial set of leaves. Seeds also contain one or two cotyledons, also called seed leaves, which serve as food storage for the tiny plant. Some seeds, corn for example, also contain additional stored food, called endosperm.

A seed gets the signal to sprout when it is exposed to the proper temperature and enough water seeps from the soil through the seed wall. (The hardness or thickness of the seed coat affects how quickly water can seep in. See Special-Needs Seeds, page 58, for ways to cope with thick seed coats.) Seeds also need oxygen to germinate, which is why it's important to plant in loose, well-drained soil or seed-starting mix that has space available for oxygen. The lack of sufficient soil oxygen is why seeds don't germinate well in compacted soil.

Once the seed absorbs enough water, the embryo begins to grow. The radicle, or root, pushes down first. Then the stem elongates. In some seeds the cotyledons stay underground (hypogeal germination), while in others they are pushed aboveground (epigeal germination). The seedling depends on the food stored in cotyledons and endosperm to fuel the germination process. Once the tiny leaves (called true leaves) contained in the embryo are exposed to light and expand, the new plant can begin to make its own food.

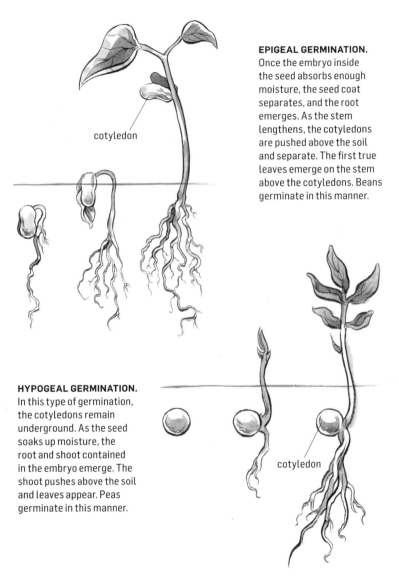

EPIGEAL GERMINATION. Once the embryo inside the seed absorbs enough moisture, the seed coat separates, and the root emerges. As the stem lengthens, the cotyledons are pushed above the soil and separate. The first true leaves emerge on the stem above the cotyledons. Beans germinate in this manner.

cotyledon

HYPOGEAL GERMINATION. In this type of germination, the cotyledons remain underground. As the seed soaks up moisture, the root and shoot contained in the embryo emerge. The shoot pushes above the soil and leaves appear. Peas germinate in this manner.

cotyledon

ANY LIFE LEFT?

Seed doesn't stay alive, or viable, forever. Old seed or improperly stored seed may germinate at a lower percentage or not at all when compared to fresh seed. (See page 33 for details on proper storage.) It's a good idea to test the germination of seed stored from a previous growing season. That way, you can buy a new supply if the seed doesn't germinate at all, or simply sow more thickly if the percentage of germination is low.

Germination testing is best for annual flowers and vegetables that sprout quickly. Because perennials and woody plants sprout much slower and often have dormancy requirements that prevent quick germination, it's often easier to sow such seeds and just see what comes up.

To test seeds of annual flowers and vegetables, you will need paper towels, zipper-type plastic bags, and, of course, the seeds to test. For best results, use strong paper towels, so they do not rip as they are folded and unfolded during the test.

1. Spread out 10 seeds, about 1 inch apart, on a damp paper towel. If there are signs of rot in the first couple of days, use a new batch of seeds and dip them in a weak bleach solution (1 part bleach to 10 parts water), then rinse them with clear water before repeating the test. This prevents fungi, which cause rot. Then spread them out on a damp paper towel. Make sure the towel is damp, but not dripping wet.

2. Fold or roll up the towel.

3. Write the name of the plant and the date on a piece of paper or a label.

4. Place the paper towel and the label in a plastic bag, close partway, and set it in a warm (65° to 70°F) place.

5. Starting in 1 week, or after the normal number of days to germination (see the seed packet for this information), unroll the towel daily or every other day to check for sprouted seedlings. Remove any seeds that show signs of rot to keep them from infecting the rest of the seeds.

If more than 7 of the seeds sprout, sow at the normal rate recommended on the packet. If less than 7 have sprouted, sow more densely to allow for the lower rate. If no seeds germinate within a week or so of the normal germination time, replace the seeds.

**GERMINATION
TESTING**

SET UP A SOWING SCHEDULE

Seed packets pile up quickly, so having a strategy for getting all the seeds sown at the right time is essential. The best sowing method and schedule varies from plant to plant — and from gardener to gardener. Scheduling also varies depending on where the garden is located, the conditions it offers, and the preferences of the gardener. For example, northern gardeners are more likely to start plants indoors to get a head start on a short growing season. Southern gardeners may cope with summer heat by starting crops indoors for spring and fall harvest.

Keep in mind that the best sowing schedules are working documents. You don't just write them out, follow them for a year, and toss them away. That's because keeping records of the vegetables or flowers you grew, when you sowed or transplanted, and what worked — or didn't — one year will help you

Ask Around

Sowing and transplant times vary by region, exposure, and even soil type. For this reason, friends and neighbors who garden can provide invaluable information on what works in your area. All gardeners sow their seeds a bit differently, so ask about when they sow or transplant different crops. Learning about what has worked for them may help improve your results.

Read Before You Plant

Seed packets from good-quality suppliers contain a wealth of valuable information, so read and hang on to them after sowing. Good suppliers provide information on growing requirements (sun/shade, soil moisture, heat tolerance), height at maturity, days to harvest or maturity, sowing recommendations (indoors/outdoors, warm vs. cool), germination specifics (planting depth, days to germination), plus recommended spacing and thinning advice. Catalogs and websites from these suppliers are also valuable sources of information.

adjust the process in future years. So whether your schedule is in a conventional journal, in a spreadsheet on your computer, or on an iPad, continue adding notes to it throughout the season. Local and site-specific notes and information are the secret to becoming a better seed-starter and gardener.

Setting up a sowing schedule will keep your seeds and seedlings coming along when you need them, and organizing your seed packets by sowing date will make it easier to find the seeds you want, when you need them. Here's how to do it:

Figure out your last spring frost date. Ask your local Cooperative Extension office; they have information on the best times to sow and transplant seedlings in your area. See Resources and Links on page 115 for tips on finding your extension office.

Sort seeds based on sowing dates. Find the recommended sowing method (direct-sow or start early indoors) and timing (commonly given in terms of weeks before the last spring frost date), usually on the back of your seed packets. For example, cabbages and marigolds are both typically started indoors 4 to 6 weeks before the last spring frost date. Count backward from your frost date to determine the sowing date. Write the sowing date on the outside of a large envelope or zip-lock bag and drop the packet into it. Also note the sowing date on your calendar as a reminder. Repeat the process with each seed packet, adding envelopes with new sowing dates as necessary.

Mark transplant times. While you're sorting seeds, also note suggested transplant times on your calendar for the various vegetables and seeds you're going to grow. You don't have to transplant on that particular day — you may not want to if the weather isn't suitable — but this gives you a handy list

SIMPLE SORTING.
Organizing seeds according to the general date when they need to be sown makes it easier to keep track of what needs to be planted, and when. It's also a good idea to separate seeds that need indoor versus outdoor sowing.

of vegetables and approximate transplant dates, right on your calendar. When sowing time arrives, refer to the seed packets themselves for exact requirements, including depth to cover or need for light or darkness.

Seed Sorting at a Glance

Use the quick-reference list below to sort seed packets into two envelopes for outdoor sowing:

Crops for Cool Conditions. These crops germinate best when the soil is cool, from 40° to 55°F.

- Arugula
- Beets
- Carrots
- Lettuce
- Mesclun mixes

Crops for Warm Conditions. These heat-loving crops sprout best when the soil is warm, 60°F and above.

- Beans (snap, bush, lima, and pole)
- Cucumbers
- Melons
- Okra
- Squash, zucchini

Crops for In-Between. The crops in this category sprout best when the soil is still on the cool side, but above 50°F. Radishes and spinach also prefer cool conditions for best growth. Sweet corn prefers warmer soil and grows well in hot weather, but can be sown once the soil reaches 50°F.

- Radishes
- Spinach
- Sweet corn

Schedule outdoor sowing. Soil temperature is the key to success with plants that are sown directly out in the garden. Lettuce and peas are cold tolerant; they germinate well in soil that is 40°F (although if the soil is too wet, the seeds may rot before they germinate). Other crops, like cucumbers, need much warmer soil. You'll find recommended germination temperatures on seed packets, in catalogs, and on the internet. For the purpose of scheduling, sort seed packets into three envelopes, one for crops that thrive in cool soil, a second for ones that need warm soil conditions to grow well, and a third for seeds that prefer conditions between the other two. See Seed Sorting at a Glance, page 27, for some common crops that fall into these categories. Start checking the soil a few weeks before the last frost date to determine when it's time to start planting the cool-season seeds. See Getting Your Garden Ready for Seeds on page 93 for more on determining when to plant.

Look for Experiments

Always be on the lookout for different methods and schedules to experiment with. Sowing a few seeds one way and a few another helps determine which way works best for you. Be sure to keep notes so you remember and use your results in future seasons.

Cycle Your Sowing

Whether you're starting seeds indoors or out, keep in mind that sowing an entire packet at one time isn't always the best option. For many crops, including all the easy crops listed on page 55, sowing a few seeds or a foot or two of row every 10 days to 2 weeks often makes more sense. Sowing in batches spreads out the harvest so that everything isn't ready to pick all at once. This especially makes sense for vegetables destined for fresh use, like lettuce. If you're planning to freeze your crop, all-at-once planting makes more sense. Heat-loving summer crops like tomatoes and peppers are generally planted all at one time. To extend the harvest on some crops — cabbage, for example — plant both early-bearing and regular-season crops. For example, early cabbage 'Farao' is ready for harvest in 64 days from transplanting, while 'Kaitlin', a late-season type selected because it stores well, takes 94 days from transplanting.

For flowers like larkspurs or zinnias, sowing in small batches means waves of color and flowers for cutting over a longer season.

PLANT IN BATCHES.
Sowing a few seeds or a foot of row every 10 days to 2 weeks helps spread out the harvest over a long season. This is especially useful for easy crops like leaf lettuce, beets, arugula, radishes, and mesclun.

SEED-GROWERS' PROBLEM SOLVER

WELL-RAISED SEEDLINGS are usually vigorous and healthy. Since most problems are easiest to nip in the bud if caught early, it pays to be on the lookout for the symptoms and problems below.

Seedlings rot at soil line and fall over. Damping-off, a fungal disease most prevalent in container-grown seedlings, is the cause, and afflicted plants cannot be saved. Seeds also can rot before they emerge from the soil. Prevent damping-off by starting with clean containers, giving seeds well-drained soil, good light, and gentle air circulation. A small fan is useful to keep air moving, but don't point it directly at seedlings; too much air movement will dry them out. Overcrowding can also cause damp, stagnant air, which fosters the fungi that cause this disease. Dusting the soil surface with sand or milled sphagnum moss helps keep the base of the seedlings dry, which helps prevent damping-off. Watering pots from below also helps keep the moisture in the soil instead of on the plants: Set pots in a tray of water, and let moisture soak upward.

DAMPING-OFF. A fungal disease that causes seedlings to rot.

Seedlings disappear. Cutworms or animal pests are the likely suspects. Cutworms are large, hairless caterpillars that hide in soil during the day. They eat seedlings entirely or chomp stems at the soil line, leaving the top of the seedling lying on the ground. Some cutworm species climb plants and eat young leaves and stems. To protect transplants, slip a 2- to 3-inch-long section of cardboard toilet paper tube (or a bottomless paper cup) over each plant as you transplant it. Before seeding a bed, rake up the surface a week before seeding to expose cutworms to birds and other predators. Where cutworms are a constant problem, make a mixture of moistened wheat bran, Bt *(Bacillus thuringiensis)*, and molasses and spread it over the seedbed before planting. Applying parasitic nematodes to the soil also helps control cutworms. (Both products are available from garden suppliers.)

Birds and Other Pests

Birds, rabbits, squirrels, and other animals pests may view your garden as a smorgasbord of delights. Place hardware cloth or bird netting over seedbeds to prevent birds from walking down the row and digging out newly planted seeds. Remove it when seedlings are still small enough to slip thorough the openings, though. Wire cages (made of 1-inch poultry wire) placed over newly seeded areas or transplants keep all but mice and voles at bay. For a vegetable garden, a fence is the best prevention against all animal pests. Ideally, line a trench around the base of the fence with poultry wire, then attach the wire to the base of the fence. Otherwise rabbits and other diggers simply go under the barrier. If birds are the major problem, protect crops with row covers or bird netting. Birds seem to avoid the flashing and movement these materials cause as they blow in the wind.

SAVING AND STORING SECRETS

COLLECTING AND SAVING SEEDS for next year's garden is an age-old tradition. Use these general guidelines to get started.

Know what you're saving. If your garden is filled with heirloom vegetables and flowers, which are open-pollinated, you'll have lots of plants to choose from. (See Seed Types and Terms on page 14 for more information.) Open-pollinated, or OP, plants are much more likely to yield seedlings that reproduce the fruit or flowers of their parent plants. Seeds collected from hybrid plants do not generally "come true." That means the seedlings do not necessarily resemble their parents, and even if they resemble them superficially, they may not carry specific disease resistance or other characteristics. Refer to your seed packets to determine whether you have hybrids or OP plants in your garden.

Seeds to start with. A good way to begin seed-saving is to start with self-pollinated plants. Plants like peas, beans, tomatoes, peppers, eggplant, and snapdragons pollinate their own flowers, so seed collected from these will come true, meaning the seeds you collect will produce plants that resemble their parents. Also, large seeds, such as those produced by marigolds, zinnias, beans, and peas, are easy to collect and handle.

Plants where wind or insects carry pollen from flower to flower are likely to produce hybrid seed, so these aren't the best choice when you're just starting out. Experienced seed-savers take steps to prevent wind or insects from carrying pollen to flowers that they want to collect seed from. They do this by growing plants away from ones that could pollinate the flowers or by protecting specific flowers with paper bags, and cross-pollinating by hand.

COLLECTING AND STORING SEEDS

In order to be viable, seed needs to mature on the plant, but it also needs to be collected as soon as it is ripe. Otherwise it will be dispersed or lost to birds or insects. Use the following steps to collect and store seeds.

1. Identify the best plants to collect seed from. That means, you want to collect seeds from the healthiest and most vigorous plants, as well as the plants that had the most flowers or fruit. Harvest mature seed pods or fruit, placing them in separate plastic or paper bags. Write the name of the plant and the date collected on the bag or on a label placed inside it.

2. Seeds of many crops, including peas and beans, are dry when they're mature. To store them, crumble the pods or break them open to remove the seeds. The seed of other crops, like tomatoes and pumpkins, is covered with fleshy fruit that needs to be removed so the seeds can be dried for storage. In this case, to save seeds, crush or cut open the fruit and put it — seeds and all — in a bowl. Cover the

fruit-and-seed mixture with water and allow it to stand for several days. Pulp rises to the surface and seeds sink to the bottom, so you can pour off the water and most of the pulp. Repeat until all of the pulp has been separated from the seeds. Spread the seeds on newspaper. Let seeds dry out for at least a week. Keep each batch of seed with its proper label during this process!

3. Place the dried seed in dry, screw-top glass jars. (A packet of silica gel or a bit of rice in each jar helps ensure that seeds stay dry.) If you have lots of seed, place each type (with its label) in a separate jar. For smaller quantities, put the seeds in labeled paper envelopes and store several batches in the same jar. Plastic prescription bottles also make good storage jars.

4. Place packaged seed in the refrigerator, to maintain a temperature between 34° and 41°F.

PART 2

STARTING SEEDS INDOORS

Gardeners everywhere start the growing season by filling containers with potting soil and sowing seeds. And whether they germinate their seedlings on windowsills, under artificial lights, in a greenhouse, or outdoors in a cold frame, the processes are basically the same. They all involve putting seeds in contact with moist, well-drained soil, then give the resulting seedlings what they need to thrive. In this section, you'll find information on the basic tools and techniques you'll need to sow seed and grow plants indoors successfully.

The essential tools couldn't be simpler. You'll need seeds, pots or other containers, flats to set them in, and potting medium (such as the Germinating Mix on page 39). You'll also need labels and a pencil or a nursery marking pen to keep track of the identity of your seedlings. In addition to these basics, consider adding a heat mat or some of the other "handy helpers" on page 48 to your arsenal. Gardeners who work away from home, or have trouble remembering to water seedlings, will enjoy using one of the germination systems available. See page 41 for more information on these handy labor-savers.

The basic techniques are simple, too. Start by figuring out the best time to plant, and then stick to your schedule. This ensures your seedlings will be about the right size when they go into the garden. (See Set Up a Sowing Schedule on page 24.) The supplies and techniques listed in this section will help ensure success.

Above all, remember that the main priority is for the seeds to get what they require to germinate. It's your job to make sure this happens. Pay attention to the details, and you'll be rewarded with a healthy crop of seedlings to plant out in the garden.

....

A Place to Pot

In addition to gathering seeds, containers, flats, labels, and a few other necessities, you'll need to find a suitable work area. Look for a spot where a bit of potting soil sprinkled about won't matter too much, and where water on tables or the floor won't damage anything. If you don't have a suitable spot in the basement or work room, consider buying a tarp to spread before you begin to fill pots. They make cleanup easy: gather up spilled soil and dump it outside in the garden.

....

GATHER YOUR GEAR

All the tools and supplies listed on the pages that follow are available from your garden center or through mail-order suppliers. Try out different containers, seed-starting mixes, and germination systems until you determine what works best for you. Even advanced gardeners continue to experiment, so plan on testing a few new options every year.

Seed-Starting Mixes

For most new gardeners, it comes as a surprise that seeds don't need rich soil to germinate. In fact, the best seed-starting medium doesn't contain fertilizer or compost at all. Feeding starts only after seedlings are up and growing. The light, firm-but-airy texture of a good seed-starting medium, plus the fact that it is sterile, helps reduce problems with seeds rotting and seedling diseases like damping-off. It also helps maintain the correct balance of moisture and air in the soil so seeds can germinate.

The easiest option is to buy premixed seed-starting medium. Or use the recipes on page 39 to mix your own from supplies purchased at your local garden center. Avoid adding ordinary garden soil to potting mixes used to germinate seeds or grow seedlings, because it contains fungi and other organisms that can cause rot and other diseases.

Selecting Containers and Flats

Seeds will happily germinate in a wide variety of containers, provided they are filled with good-quality seed-starting medium and have holes in the bottom for water to drain away. Here are some of your options:

Purchased pots and packs. While you'll probably end up needing several sizes for seedlings as they grow, 3½-inch pots are a useful, standard size. Square pots are more space-efficient than round ones. Cell packs, with either 1½- or 2-inch cells, are also useful for smaller annuals.

Recycled pots and packs. Every gardener has a supply of pots from previous seasons. (If you're a new gardener, ask gardening friends if they have pots to spare.) Wash pots before reusing them. Ideally you should sterilize them by dipping in a 10 percent bleach solution (1 part bleach added to 9 parts water). Air-dry before refilling.

HOMES FOR SEEDS. Many different containers work for germinating seeds, but sticking to one or two types makes seedling care easier, since they will need watering on similar schedules.

Make-It-Yourself Mixes

To mix the recipes below, use a large bucket or tub. (A tarp may help contain the mess!) If you intend to transplant seedlings from small flats or pots into larger ones before planting in the garden, use the Germinating Mix recipe, or start with purchased seed-starting mix. When sowing seeds in pots that will hold plants until they are transplanted to the garden, use regular commercial potting soil or the Potting Mix for Seedlings recipe below, because they contain nutrients seedlings need to grow.

All the ingredients listed below can be purchased from a local garden center or via the Internet. Note: Coir fiber is made from coconut husk fibers. It's a substitute for peat, which is a mined product.

Germinating Mix
- 1 part perlite or vermiculite
- 1 part milled sphagnum moss, well-screened compost, coir fiber, or peat

Potting Mix for Seedlings
- 1 part well-screened compost
- 1 part vermiculite

Alternate Potting Mix for Seedlings
- 1 or 2 parts ordinary commercial potting soil
- 1 part perlite
- 1 part well-screened compost, leaf mold, or coir fiber

Plantable containers. Pots that can go right into the ground are perfect for fussy seedlings, though some gardeners like to use plantable pots for all transplants, not just the fussy ones. The best-known plantable pots are made of peat and wood fiber, but now ones made from composted cow manure as well as coir (coconut fiber) are also available. Once these pots are moist, plant roots can grow right through the sides and into the soil. As the containers are biodegradable, seedlings can be set in the ground, pot and all.

Plantable pellets. These consist of small buttons of compressed seed-starting medium, roughly ⅜ inch tall and 1¾ inches wide. They offer another easy option for growing seedlings that can be planted in the garden, pot and all. Traditionally they were made of peat, but pellets made of composted cow manure are also available. Soak them in water to expand the pellet, then sow a seed in the top.

Found containers. Any container that can hold seed-starting medium and is the right size can be used to start seeds. Yogurt cups and paper coffee cups are popular choices. Just poke drainage holes in the bottom of each container before filling and sowing.

Homes for Pots

You'll also want flats or trays in which to place pots or six-packs. If you'll be germinating your seeds in a place that can get wet, flats with slits in the bottom to allow for drainage are best. Otherwise, look for shallow trays that hold water and won't drip.

Self-Watering Seed Starters

These simple systems make it easy to keep soil perfectly moist, not too damp and not too dry. If you didn't have luck with previous attempts at starting seeds because seeds dried out or drowned, investing in one of these systems can guarantee success and increase your confidence. If you're headed off on vacation, these systems will keep your seedlings watered while you're away. Make sure you purchase one that can be reused just by refilling the seed tray with new mix.

EASY AUTOMATIC WATERING. Most seed companies offer seed-starting systems where honeycomb-style seed containers sit on top of a water reservoir. An absorbent sheet or blanket wicks water from the reservoir to the soil mix, keeping seedlings perfectly watered as long as the reservoir remains filled.

Pots for Fussy Seedlings

Transplanting seedlings to the garden disturbs roots, and some plants cope with this better than others. Parsley and many vegetables such as melons, carrots, and cucumbers are often sown directly in the garden because they don't transplant well. Annuals such as California poppies (*Eschscholzia californica*), nasturtiums (*Tropaeolum majus*), larkspur (*Consolida ajacis*), and wishbone flowers (*Torenia fournieri*) have similar problems. Fortunately, planning ahead helps. Use these tips to get fussy seedlings off to a good start:

- If you want to start difficult-to-transplant seeds indoors, sow in individual pots, not flats, so you don't have to separate small seedlings when transplanting.

- Use plantable containers, newspaper pots, or soil blocks (page 45) to minimize transplanting shock.

- Schedule carefully. Don't start larger vegetables like squash, melons, or cucumbers too early. Otherwise, they outgrow their pots, which will limit their growth rate and make transplanting more difficult.

- Handle difficult-to-transplant seedlings very carefully. Try to minimize root disturbance when transplanting them.

Stick to a Size

It's a good idea to sow all your seeds in the same size container, or maybe stick to only two different sizes. That way, all your seedlings will need watering on the same basic schedule.

PENNY-PINCHING NEWSPAPER POTS

Using strips of newspaper, homemade plantable pots are inexpensive and easy to make. You can buy one of the wooden forms for making them (from mail-order garden supply companies), or use a can or other container as a form to make larger pots. Here's how to make them:

1. Cut or tear strips of newspaper. Use strips about 3½ inches wide by 10 inches long to make pots with a standard wooden form. Use strips that are 4 inches by 10 inches for wrapping around small (6-ounce) tomato paste cans. Experiment with the correct height and length if using another form. In most cases, the finished pots should be about 2½ to 3 inches tall, with enough of the strip left over to cover the bottom.

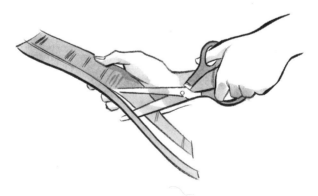

2. Wrap the paper tightly around the form, lining up one side of the paper with the top of the form or partway down the can. Let the excess stick out past the bottom of the form.

3. Crush or fold the paper across the bottom of the form or can to create the bottom of the pot.

4. Slide the newspaper off the form or can, then fill with moist seed-starting medium and place the pot in a flat. Pots should touch to help keep them moist and tightly rolled.

MAKING SUPER-SIMPLE SOIL BLOCKS

These "pots" consist of soil alone. Transplants don't have to push their roots through the sides of a plantable pot and so establish quickly and easily. While you do have to make an initial investment in a block-maker, once you have one, soil blocks are less expensive than plantable pellets, plus you don't have to bother with pots or flimsy market packs.

To make them, you'll need a special soil block maker. A 2-inch blocker is a good size to start out. You also need special soil mix; use the recipe below, or buy premade mix. Don't use ordinary potting soil, since the resulting blocks will not hold together well.

Practice a few times, and don't be afraid to toss the first few test blocks back into the bin. There is a knack to making blocks, but learning how is well worth the trouble. Finished blocks should be firm and will hold together on their own.

Simple Soil Block Mix

- 4 parts sphagnum peat moss
- 1 part screened compost or worm castings
- ⅛ part coarse rinsed sand (sandblasting or builders sand is fine)
- 1 handful of limestone or rock powder

1. Place blocking mix in a large tub and add water until the mix is about the consistency of oatmeal. Let it set for at least 45 minutes, to make sure all the ingredients are moist.

2. Jam the blocking mold into the mix, remove, then eject the blocks into a tray or flat that has holes or mesh in the bottom.

3. Space blocks about ⅛ inch apart, so that exposure to air will "prune" any roots that grow out from each block.

Handy Helpers

It's certainly possible to germinate seeds successfully with limited equipment, but some of the following items are worthwhile additions to any indoor seed-starting operation.

Heat mat. Seed for most vegetables and annual flowers germinates best when temperatures are between 68° and 86°F. Soil temperatures are key here, as seedlings are generally sturdier if air temperatures remain slightly lower. A heat mat keeps soil 10° to 20°F above the surrounding air. It's the easiest way to keep soil warm, which speeds germination and encourages rapid root growth and sturdy plants. (A heat mat is also a must-have for rooting cuttings!) Because pots sit directly on the mat, there is no heat loss. Most are made of heavy-gauge polyvinyl; rubber heat mats are also available but are more expensive. They are designed to withstand damp conditions and spilled

TOASTY ROOTS. An energy-efficient heat mat warms the soil slightly, which speeds germination and root growth.

water. (Pots should still be set in flats on the heat mat to minimize spills when you're watering). The mats are available in various sizes, which accommodate one, two, or four standard-size flats.

Humidity covers. Seed companies sell a variety of clear plastic domes to go over seed flats and provide beneficial humidity for seedlings. It's easy and inexpensive to make a simple humidity tent out of plastic dry-cleaner bags and wire coat hangers.

SOWING ONE BY ONE.
Spreading seeds out one at a time can be a tedious process. A simple seed handler is an easy solution that makes sowing all sizes of seed a simple matter.

Seed sowers or handlers. Spreading seeds out thinly can be tricky, especially when they are small. A variety of simple tools make it easy to sow seeds thinly, two or three to a pot. A hand-held seed sower is inexpensive and makes handling seeds a cinch. Place seeds in the round portion, replace the clear plastic cap, and adjust the cap so the proper size hole lines up with the spout. Then tap seeds in place.

Lights. Even if you have plenty of bright, sunny windowsills, consider supplemental lighting; it makes growing healthy seedlings much easier. Even with sunny windowsills, the early spring light is too weak to grow sturdy seedlings. One ordinary fluorescent shop light provides sufficient illumination for two standard flats. See Let There Be Lights below for more information.

Let There Be Lights

Good light is essential for raising robust, stocky, vigorous seedlings, so it pays to do a bit of planning to make sure you can provide adequate light. Inadequate light results in tall, spindly seedlings. While newly sown flats don't need light, once seedlings appear, they need fairly intense light in order to thrive. Use the following guidelines to provide your seedlings with what they need.

Evaluate your windowsills. Bright, east- or west-facing windowsills may provide sufficient light to grow compact, vigorous seedlings. Depending on what region of the country you live in, south-facing windows may be too sunny and hot, which means seedlings will need watering more often and are prone to scorching. If windowsills are too narrow, install shelf brackets and boards, bookcases, or other furniture under them. Protect furniture with plastic to prevent moisture damage. Even with bright windows, days are short in wintertime, so seedlings will likely need supplemental light for best growth.

More is generally better. Seedlings started indoors need about 16 hours of light per day; 14 hours is acceptable for good growth. (This is a major reason that supplemental lighting is so beneficial to seedlings.) If plants are growing in a cool location, seedlings can manage with 12 hours per day. Plants grow best with no more than 18 hours of light per day.

Use artificial lights. Fluorescent lights are ideal for raising good seedlings. While special plant grow lights are available, they are expensive. Seedlings raised under ordinary fluorescent lights are just about as healthy and stocky as those grown under fancy bulbs. (Use new bulbs, not old ones, since they provide significantly more light.) The secret to growing really sturdy seedlings is to mount the lights using chains and S-hooks. That way, it's easy to adjust the distance between the growing seedlings and the lights. Keep the topmost leaves of the seedlings 3 inches below the lights for the first few weeks. After that, adjust the lights so they are 4 to 6 inches above the topmost leaves of the plants.

BRIGHT IS BEST. For the sturdiest seedlings, adjust lights to keep them close to the topmost leaves of the plants.

What Goes Where?

If you have lots of pots and loads of space, this may not be a question you'll have to ponder, but most gardeners have to cope with the quandary of too many seeds and not enough space. Use these tips to help you make the best use of your space.

Sow densely. For space-efficient germination, sow many seeds per pot or tray (try to space them out over the entire surface). Then transplant seedlings to individual containers when they have at least two sets of true leaves. This is a good way to make the most of limited space on heat mats and under humidity covers. Once seedlings germinate, it is essential to thin them and then transplant to individual pots, to give them room to grow. Otherwise, the overcrowded seedlings compete with one another, get lanky, and become more prone to disease. See Thinning Seedlings (page 65) and Potting On (page 70) for more on these techniques.

Sow singly. Some gardeners hate fussing with tiny seedlings. If your goal is to avoid the need to transplant until seeds are moved to the garden, sow 3 or 4 seeds per pot. Remove all but the strongest 1 or 2 seedlings when they have about two sets of true leaves.

SEEDS PER POT. To avoid transplanting, sow 3 or 4 seeds per pot, then thin to one seedling. Or sow densely and move seedlings on when they are still small.

SOWING YOUR SEED

ONCE YOU HAVE SEEDS and necessary equipment in hand, and your calendar says it's time, the fun begins. Time to start filling pots and sowing seeds! Keep your sowing schedule handy, and make notes as you plant seeds. Records from previous years about what you sowed (and when) are extremely useful for determining the best planting dates and timing for your garden.

Moisten Before You Fill

For best results, moisten the germinating or potting mix *before* filling pots. Commercial mixes can be very difficult to wet thoroughly, especially in individual pots, and dry pockets in the mix can impair germination. The day before you intend to sow, fill a large bucket with enough mix for the day's planting. Add plenty of warm water, then stir until all the ingredients are moist. If you can't premoisten the day before, at least do it a couple of hours before sowing. This allows time for moisture to permeate the entire mix and eliminates dry pockets.

SOWING, STEP BY STEP

After premoistening your germinating mix, read your seed packets to determine whether seeds have any special germination requirements, such as needing light or darkness (see Special-Needs Seeds, page 58). Then use the following steps to sow your seeds:

SOWING, STEP BY STEP, continued

1. Fill each container with pre-moistened germinating or potting mix. As you fill, tap the container on the work surface to settle it, then *gently* firm the mix with your fingers. The potting mix should be about ½ inch below the rim of the pot.

2. Sprinkle seeds thinly over the surface of the potting mix, or sow 3 or 4 seeds in the center, depending on whether you are planning to transplant later. Use a hand-held seed sower, or place seeds on a small piece of folded paper and tap gently to spread them. Plant large seeds and pelletized seeds individually.

3. Use moistened, sifted potting mix to dust over the seeds to a depth just barely equal to thickness of seeds. For very tiny seeds, or seeds that require light for germination, just press seeds onto the surface of the medium.

Easy Vegetables for Starting Indoors

The crops on this list have different schedules, so check seed packets to determine when to sow. All are fairly easy to start from seeds indoors.

- Broccoli
- Brussels sprouts
- Cabbage
- Cauliflower
- Cucumbers
- Leaf lettuce
- Leeks
- Okra
- Onions
- Peppers
- Pumpkins/winter squash
- Swiss chard
- Tomatoes
- Zucchini/summer squash

4. Label each container as you go with the name of the plant and the date sown. Set each container in a tray of water, allow the water to soak the soil from below, then move it to another tray and let it drain. Or moisten each container with mist from a spray bottle. Don't use a watering can or faucet, as even a gentle stream of water can wash seeds away.

5. Set containers where the seeds will germinate. Flats don't need sun until seedlings appear, but it's often easiest to set them where they will ulti- mately be growing.

After sowing, keep the germinating mix evenly moist but not wet. Remember that seeds need a balance between water and air. Cover flats with a humidity cover, or cover loosely with clear plastic. Remove the humidity cover as soon as seedlings appear. See From Seeds to Seedlings on page 64 for details on giving germinating seeds and young seedlings what they'll need to grow.

Gentle Pressure

Seeds need to take up moisture from the seed-starting medium in order to germinate. After sowing, press the medium down gently to provide good seed-to-soil contact. Pressing eliminates air pockets, which can prevent water uptake. Don't press too hard, though, since seeds also need air, which they get through smaller air pockets in the medium. Gentle pressure ensures that they receive the balance of air and water they require.

Easy Annuals for Starting Indoors

Opinions vary on which annuals are the best choices to grow from seed started indoors. The following are among the easiest.

- Ageratum, floss flower (*Ageratum houstonianum*) •
- Celosia, cockscomb (*Celosia argentea*)
- Cleome, spider flower (*Cleome hassleriana*)
- Coleus (*Solenostemon scutellarioides*) •
- Cosmos (*Cosmos* species)
- Impatiens and garden balsam (*Impatiens* species) ✳
- Marigolds (*Tagetes* species)
- Nicotianas, flowering tobaccos (*Nicotiana* species) •
- Salvias (*Salvia* species) •
- Snapdragons (*Antirrhinum majus*) ••✦
- Statice (*Limonium sinuatum*)
- Sweet alyssum (*Lobularia maritima*) •
- Zinnias (*Zinnia* species) ✚

- • Needs light to germinate; press seed onto the surface of the soil.
- ✦ Best grown in cool temperatures, 50° to 55°F.
- ✚ Can be fussy about transplanting; see Pots for Fussy Seedlings on page 42.
- ✳ Cover seeds very lightly.

SPECIAL-NEEDS SEEDS

WHILE MOST COMMON SEEDS GERMINATE readily, some have a more complex dormancy that prevents them from sprouting unless certain conditions are met. Seeds may have very hard seed coats that prevent water uptake, they may need light to germinate, or they may require a period of moisture and cool temperatures in order to sprout. In nature, such requirements prevent seeds from germinating during adverse weather, when seedlings have little or no chance of surviving. While it would be great if every seed germinated right away, ferreting out what special conditions unusual seeds need to germinate is all part of the fun. These are the types of seed treatments you may need to provide.

Scarification. Very hard seed coats can prevent the intake of water and thus prevent sprouting. Scarification is the process of nicking, sanding, or otherwise wearing down the seed coat to hasten germination. To scarify, rub seeds on coarse sandpaper or carefully nick the seed coat with a knife or razor blade. Take care to cut or sand off only the seed coat and not the embryo itself. Soaking seed for 12 to 24 hours in warm water is an alternative to scarifying. Seeds that require scarification include morning glories (*Ipomoea* species), baptisias or false indigoes (*Baptisia* species), and lupines (*Lupinus* species).

Light or darkness for germination. Read seed packets to find out whether the seed you're sowing requires either light or darkness for germination. For seeds that require light to germinate — including lettuce, ageratums (*Ageratum* species), begonias (*Begonia* species), browallias (*Browallia* species), impatiens (*Impatiens* species), and petunias (*Petunia* species) — just press the seeds onto the surface of the seed-starting medium and do not cover with additional medium. If the seeds are extremely small, it is often best to sow on the surface and cover the flats or pots with plastic until seeds germinate.

Cover seeds that require darkness with germinating mix. Seeds that need darkness to germinate include calendulas or pot marigolds (*Calendula* species), centaureas (*Centaurea* species), annual phlox (*Phlox* species), and verbenas (*Verbena* species).

Stratification

Some seeds, most commonly perennials, trees, and shrubs, require one or more periods of moist storage at cool or warm temperatures (or a sequence of specific temperatures) in order to sprout. This moist storage is called stratification. With other seeds, stratification speeds germination but isn't required. Seeds requiring cool-moist stratification in order to sprout are most common.

Cool-moist stratification. Expose seeds to temperatures of 32° to 45°F for a period of 1 to 3 months (duration depends on the species).

Warm-moist stratification. Expose seeds to temperatures of 68° to 86°F for the required period.

Complex dormancy. Plants can require almost any combination of cool-moist and warm-moist stratification. Read each seed packet, or search the Internet for specific requirements of particular species. (Resources and Links on page 115 lists sites with databases of germination requirements.)

Merely storing unplanted seeds in the refrigerator or in a warm spot won't satisfy stratification requirements, because the seeds need to be exposed to moisture at the same time to break down the dormancy factors that prevent germination. (See Seed Dormancy, page 61.) If the seeds require a period of cool, moist conditions, place the pot in the refrigerator for the recommended length of time, then move the pot to a warm spot for sprouting. For seeds with more complicated requirements — some need a period of warm temperatures followed by cool temperatures, then warm again for sprouting — simply

STRATIFY TO SPROUT.
Refrigerator space and seeds planted in pots or packed in barely damp medium in a plastic bag is all it takes to satisfy most stratification requirements.

move the pots from place to place to give them the temperatures they need. Keep pots loosely covered with plastic to make sure the seed-starting medium stays evenly moist throughout the stratification process.

Or, mix seeds with a small amount of moist (not wet) vermiculite, peat, or sand in a plastic bag. Then move the bag(s) from place to place to satisfy the seeds' stratification requirements. Once the requirements are met, you don't have to separate seed from the vermiculite, peat, or sand — just sow the contents of the bag by spreading the mix on the surface of a container filled with germinating medium.

Regardless of how you handle stratification, write the sowing date and stratification schedule on the label for each plant. You'll also need to keep track of the schedule on your gardening calendar, so pots get moved from one spot to the other as required. See Perennials from Seed (page 74) and Pregerminating (page 62) for two other easy ways to handle seeds that need stratification.

Seed Dormancy

Seed dormancy prevents seeds from sprouting at the wrong time in their natural environment. For example, seeds that ripen in late fall and sprout right away will likely be killed by cold winter weather. Seeds that have a stratification requirement won't sprout until the following spring, when chances are better that seedlings will survive.

PREGERMINATING, STEP BY STEP

Some gardeners choose to pregerminate (presprout) seeds before planting them. There are three main reasons why you might do this. First, it's a way to get an extra head start on the growing season. It also gives gardeners extra control over the sprouting process, especially when dealing with expensive or hard-to-find seeds. Finally, pregerminating makes it easy to accommodate stratification requirements, since a damp paper towel provides the moisture required for stratification to occur. Bags are also easier to move and take up less space. The process for pregerminating is identical to that for testing seed viability (as described in Any Life Left? on page 22). You can use barely damp paper towels, but many gardeners swear that coffee filters make it possible to get the perfect amount of moisture, and therefore believe they're the best way to pregerminate.

Follow the steps below to pregerminate seeds.

1. Moisten a paper towel or coffee filter and wring out all the excess moisture. (It should be just damp, not wet.) Fold the towel in half, then place seeds on half the towel.

2. Fold the top of the towel over the portion covered with seeds, and place it in a partially closed ziplock bag. Use a separate bag for each type of seed, and enclose a label with the plant name and seed-sowing date in each bag. Set the bag in a warm spot (65° to 70°F). Check every few days for signs of germination.

3. Carefully remove seedlings as they appear and pot them up in containers of premoistened potting mix. Moist mix is essential, since dry mix will pull moisture from the tiny seedlings and kill them.

FROM SEEDS TO SEEDLINGS

Once your seeds are sown, set the flats in the growing area you have selected — in a window, under lights in a basement or spare room, or in a greenhouse. Most germinate quickly and reliably. Your work begins once seedlings appear, since it takes care and attention to detail to keep them growing well. Here is what your seedlings need:

Ample light. Though most seeds don't need light to sprout, seedlings require ample light to grow into sturdy, robust plants, so it's easiest to place pots or flats of sown seeds under lights. If you're starting sun-loving vegetables, consider supplementing natural light with artificial light. Even if you have a bright window, days are short and the light is weak in late winter and early spring, so seedlings may not receive enough light without a boost.

You don't need a sunny window; you can grow great seedlings under artificial lights. Set up the lights to allow you to adjust the distance between the topmost leaves and the lights as the seedlings grow. Use a timer to turn the lights on and off automatically. If plants grow tall and spindly, they are not receiving enough light. If the leaves are turned down or look scorched, the lights are too close to the leaves. See Let There Be Lights on page 50 for more on providing seedlings with the light they need to grow.

Consistent temperature. Temperatures between 65° and 70°F satisfy most seedlings, although others need cooler or warmer conditions. Check seed packets, or the Internet for

Thinning Seedlings

Thinning is one of the hardest things gardeners have to do. Eliminating healthy seedlings just seems cruel and wasteful. However, overcrowded seedlings are likely to be lanky and weak, and they never reach their full potential. So, once seedlings have four true leaves, it's time to thin — or time to transplant to individual pots. If you have sown in small pots, with several seeds per pot, use sharp nail scissors to clip off all but the healthiest seedling in the pot. (Some gardeners leave two, and that's fine as well.) Even after thinning, most seedlings will need transplanting into larger pots to give them room to grow healthy root systems before transplanting outdoors. (See Potting On, page 70.)

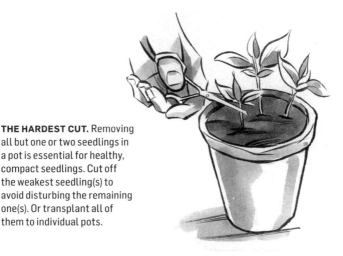

THE HARDEST CUT. Removing all but one or two seedlings in a pot is essential for healthy, compact seedlings. Cut off the weakest seedling(s) to avoid disturbing the remaining one(s). Or transplant all of them to individual pots.

recommendations. Once you determine the best temperature for growing your seedlings, try to keep the temperature fairly consistent. In general, the temperature can dip by about 10°F at night. Seedlings exposed to scorching sun during the afternoon hours and chilly temperatures at night will not be as robust as ones grown in a spot where the temperature remains relatively steady.

If you are using a heat mat to help speed germination, you can unplug it after your seeds have sprouted. Once seedlings appear and are growing strongly, you can move them off the heat mat to make space for more germinating seeds.

Even moisture. The key to healthy, happy seedlings is keeping the seed-starting medium evenly moist: never too dry and never soaking wet. Get in the habit of regularly sticking a finger into the soil in pots and flats. You'll quickly be able to tell if the soil is too wet, too dry, or just right. You can also easily judge moisture by lifting up the pots or flats: wet soil leads to heavy pots and flats, dry soil to lightweight ones. By lifting pots or flats regularly, you'll soon be able to tell what needs watering.

....

Cold Frames for Seed-Starting

Cold frames are rectangular, boxlike structures that provide cool greenhouse-like conditions. They are handy structures, especially in spring when space for growing seedlings is quickly filled to overflowing. Use them to start seedlings that prefer cool weather, including pansies, cabbage family plants such as broccoli, and many perennials. They are also ideal for hardening off transplants before they go into the garden.

HANDY STRUCTURES. Cold frames are useful for starting cool-weather crops and for hardening off transplants. For best results, install a solar-powered or electric vent to moderate temperatures automatically.

A cold frame can be a permanent structure or it can be portable, so the frame can be moved to a shady spot for germinating crops for the fall garden in summer. There are many designs available. With a quick look through garden supply catalogs or a search of the Internet, you'll find plans for build-it-yourself frames using recycled windows, and models that are ready to set up in the yard as soon as you unpack them. Set them up facing south for maximum heat collection, as cold frames depend on sun for heat. You can also add heating cables to provide warmer temperatures for plants.

All models need venting. Temperatures can rise very quickly inside them and fry seedlings on sunny winter days. Manual vents that prop open the top are fine if you're around during the daytime. A solar-powered or electric vent that raises the top automatically to control the interior temperature is more convenient, especially if you work away from home.

There are a couple of ways to water seedlings. Watering from the bottom is one of the best, especially for tiny seedlings that are easily dislodged. Bottom watering is also good for plants — such as basil, petunias, and cabbage — that are prone to damping-off. Simply set pots in a container of water and let moisture seep upward. Lift them up and move them back to their flats once the soil at the top of the pot is damp. Obviously, this can be a time-consuming process. Many gardeners water by tipping a gentle stream of water out of a bottle or other container. There are hose nozzles that deliver a fine mist that doesn't damage seedlings. Avoid flooding pots with a strong stream of water, since this can wash seeds away and dislodge seedlings.

Tepid water is best, since cold water can shock plants. This is especially true for peppers, eggplant, okra, and similar heat-loving plants. Keep in mind that plants growing in a warm house with dry air need watering frequently — as often as every other day.

Good air circulation. Once seedlings appear, adequate air circulation becomes more important than high humidity. Remove humidity covers once seedlings appear, but be extra vigilant about monitoring soil moisture during this time, since changing the humidity level changes the watering schedule. Check daily to see if pots need watering. If you're going to be away from home during the day, water in the morning and *loosely* cover seedlings for the first day or so. (Make sure air can get in from all sides.) If the soil is too wet, uncover the plants for several hours to help it dry it a little before re-covering. Small fans are very helpful for ensuring adequate air circulation, especially in greenhouses or other areas that are warm and damp. Be sure to point them in such a way that they do not blow directly on seedlings, since constant wind will desiccate seedlings.

Fertilizer in moderation. Seedlings that germinate in germinating mix need to receive small doses of fertilizer as soon as the first true leaves develop. Most seed-starting mixes contain no soil and are composed primarily of composted bark or peat; unless the package specifies otherwise, you can assume that it will supply few if any nutrients. Liquid fertilizers are easiest to use; fish emulsion and compost tea are also good organic choices. Whatever fertilizer you use, mix it into the water

TURN THEM AROUND.
Seedlings grow toward their light source, which isn't a problem if artificial lights are hanging directly overhead. Plants growing in a window will need to be turned around every couple of days to ensure straight, even growth.

before watering from the bottom or from the top. If you have very hard water, consider using rainwater or bottled water for seedlings. Read the package directions, and mix the fertilizer at half the strength recommended, since stronger dilutions can burn seedlings. Feed weekly for the first three weeks. Switch to full-strength fertilizer after that, feeding every 10 days to two weeks.

If you transplant into a potting mix that contains compost or other nutrients, your seedlings may not need to be fertilized for several weeks. Begin feeding if the color of the leaves begins to look pale.

POTTING ON

FOR HEALTHY PERFORMANCE IN THE GARDEN, seedlings need to grow steadily from germination onward. Overcrowded roots, sudden exposure to cold temperatures, and nutritional disorders are some of the factors that can check growth and cause transplant shock. Whenever you move seedlings to a larger pot (called "potting on"), or separate ones that were sown densely in a tray, it is important to minimize stress on the plants and keep them growing despite the disruption.

TIMELY TRANSPLANTING, STEP BY STEP

Transplanting seedlings to individual pots reduces overcrowding and competition, and keeps seedlings growing well. It also keeps them from shading each other out and getting spindly due to lack of light. To transplant, start by filling pots half full with premoistened potting mix, then use the steps below.

Once you've finished the transplanting process, set newly moved plants into a flat, add a humidity cover, and set the flat in a bright spot (but out of direct sunlight) for a few days while the seedlings recover. Check daily to make sure the soil remains evenly moist, but not wet. Gradually expose seedlings to more light and less humidity (by removing the cover for progressively longer periods over several days).

1. Fill a new pot with moistened potting mix. Tip a seedling out of its pot. Use a pencil or the point of a plastic plant label to gently separate the roots and top growth. Pressing gently on the rootball between seedlings can also help to separate seedlings.

2. Make a hole in the potting mix with a pencil to accommodate the roots. In most cases, you'll want to set seedlings at the same depth they were growing in their previous pots. Tomatoes, however, will grow roots along the upper stem; set them so the soil comes to just below the lowest pair of leaves.

3. Pick up a seedling, holding by a leaf, and set it into the hole you've made in the new pot. Gently spread the roots out over the potting mix as much as possible using a plastic label or a pencil.

4. Sprinkle more moistened mix into the pot around the seedling until the pot is full. Firm the mix very gently. To minimize shock, water each seedling as you move it, and then let it drain. Either mist transplants with a spray bottle, or set pots in a tray of room-temperature water and let the water soak upward to the surface. Then drain thoroughly. Watering from below is more time consuming, but it helps prevent damping-off and other fungal diseases.

PERENNIALS FROM SEED

IN GENERAL, PERENNIALS TAKE A LITTLE bit more patience to grow from seed than annual flowers do, but that's no reason to shy away from growing them. Some sprout as quickly and reliably as annuals. The ones listed under Easy Perennials and Biennials from Seed on page 78 are the best choices for beginning seed-starters. Other popular perennials like columbines (*Aquilegia* species) and many woodland wildflowers need special treatment in order for seed to germinate. (See Special-Needs Seeds on page 58 for the finicky treatments some perennials require.) Fortunately, it's fairly easy to accommodate these requirements using one of the methods outlined below.

Finding out exactly what special treatment a particular seed needs involves a little sleuthing. Commercially packaged seed usually explains any germination requirements on the packet. If your seed comes from a friend or another source, try one of the databases listed under Resources and Links on page 115. Or search the Internet for recommendations, using the botanical name of the plant plus "germination."

Method One: Simply Sowing

Perennials that germinate quickly without the need for special treatments are easy. Just treat them like annuals. Sow the seed in pots and germinate it either on a heat mat or in a cooler spot, depending on the species involved and the directions on the seed packet. Even perennials that require a period of stratification can be sown in pots of premoistened germinating mix. For these, write the length of the stratification period on the plant label, so you know when the seed is ready for germination. Place pots that need a period of cold treatment in the refrigerator for the required length of time. If a plant needs a warm-moist period before a cold-moist one, set the pots in a warm spot for the required period before moving them to the refrigerator.

Method Two: Pregerminating

An avid seed-sower can easily fill up a small refrigerator with sown pots of perennials. Unless you have a spare refrigerator, a good alternative is pregerminating seed in plastic bags. Using damp paper towels or coffee filters, follow the steps under Pregerminating on page 62.

Be sure to write the plant name, date sown, and the stratification schedule on a label and place it inside the bag. Or, write the name, date, and schedule on the outside of the plastic bag with a permanent marker.

Place the bags in an area where they receive the proper temperature — the refrigerator, the basement, the kitchen counter, or whatever you have. Check regularly to make sure the paper towels or filters don't dry out; spritz those that do with water.

When seedlings appear, pot them up in premoistened potting mix. Move them to a spot with good light so they won't get leggy.

Method Three: Germinating Perennials Outdoors

One of the easiest ways to handle perennials is to sow seeds in pots, then set the pots outdoors in a nursery area where they can sprout on their own schedule. To germinate perennials this way, just sow seed in pots whenever it is available. Midwinter is fine but so is midsummer, if that's when your seed order arrives, but you can also sow seed in summer or fall if that's when you can collect ripe seed from a plant in a friend or neighbor's garden. In fact, sowing seeds as soon as you collect them is often the best approach for native wildflowers and other perennials, because fresh seed often germinates much more quickly and easily than packaged seeds from a seed company does. After sowing, mulch the pots with very fine gravel. The gravel will make seeds less likely to wash out of the pot, keep the soil from washing away, and improve drainage.

Turkey grit, available from agricultural supply stores, is ideal, as is aquarium gravel. (Buy the tiny, uncolored stones, not the colored gravel.) Be sure to label each pot with the name of the plant and the date sown.

Set the pots outside in a protected spot. Pick a spot in partial shade that's protected from wind. The east side of a building is ideal, but any spot that receives morning sun and afternoon shade, or all-day dappled shade, is fine. Look for a spot that's handy, so you can easily check on pots periodically. You need to be able to water pots in summer, so access to a hose is also beneficial.

When treated this way, seeds that need simple cool-moist stratification often germinate in spring once warmer weather

Shrubs, Trees, and Vines from Seed

If you're feeling adventurous, try starting trees, shrubs, and vines from seed. Some germinate readily, though many more need a bit of patience. Seed of trees, shrubs, and vines — collectively called woody plants — commonly require treatments such as scarification and cool-moist or warm-moist stratification to germinate.

Sow seed of woody plants in pots and set them in a protected spot outdoors. Or plant them directly into a nursery bed. Give them plenty of time to germinate — plan to keep looking after your pots at least two years. Cover pots with wire mesh to keep rodents from feasting on the tasty seeds.

arrives. You need to be patient, though, because some seeds take a year or more to germinate. Just check fairly regularly, water as necessary, and pull any weeds that appear.

Since small seedlings are easily lost in garden beds, plan on transplanting perennial seedlings to larger pots and growing them on before transplanting to the garden. Or move them to a special nursery bed until they attain enough size to withstand the rigors of the garden. See Nursery Beds on page 89 for more information.

Easy Perennials and Biennials from Seed

It's fun to grow perennials and biennials from seed, especially if you try easy ones for your first efforts. All of the selections listed here germinate in about 2 weeks, unless otherwise noted. Any special treatment is listed for those that need it. After planting, keep pots at 65° to 70°F until seeds sprout.

Perennials

- Achilleas, yarrows (*Achillea filipendulina, A. millefolium*) ●
- Alliums, ornamental onions (*Allium caeruleum, A. schoenoprasum,* and *A. senescens*)
- Anthemis, golden marguerite (*Anthemis tinctoria*)
- Balloon flower (*Platycodon grandiflorus*) Germination takes from 15 to 30 days or more, so be patient.
- Baptisias, false indigoes (*Baptisia* species) ◆
- Campions, catchflies (*Lychnis* species)
- Centaureas, knapweeds (*Centaurea* species)
- Coreopsis (*Coreopsis grandiflora, C. lanceolata*)
- Culver's root (*Veronicastrum virginicum*) ✤
- Cupid's dart (*Catananche caerulea*)
- Dianthus, pinks (*Dianthus* species)
- Flax (*Linum flavum, L. perenne*)
- Foxgloves (*Digitalis* species) ●
- Gaillardias, blanket flowers (*Gaillardia* species)

- Hardy hibiscus, rose mallow (*Hibiscus coccineus, H. moscheutos*) Sow at 70° to 75°F.
- Hardy ice plants (*Delosperma* species)
- Hollyhock (*Alcea rosea*) ✚ Biennial or short-lived perennial.
- Lupines (*Lupinus* species) ✚ ◆
- Moss campion, autumn catchfly (*Silene acaulis, S. schafta*)
- Purple coneflowers (*Echinacea* species) ✚
- Red valerian, Jupiter's beard (*Centranthus ruber*)
- Red-hot pokers (*Kniphofia* species) ✚
- Rudbeckias, black-eyed Susans (*Rudbeckia* species) ✚
- Salvias (*Salvia* species)
- Veronicas, speedwells (*Veronica* species) ● ✚

Biennials

- Canterbury bells (*Campanula medium*)
- Foxglove (*Digitalis purpurea*)
- Gloriosa daisy (*Rudbeckia hirta*)
- Money plant (*Lunaria annua*)
- Violets and pansies (*Viola* species)

● Needs light; do not cover seeds.
◆ Soak in hot water for 24 hours before sowing.
✚ If no seedlings appear after a month at 65 to 70°F, cold-stratify for 3 to 4 weeks.

MOVING PLANTS TO YOUR GARDEN

Once days lengthen and temperatures warm, it's time to move seedlings out into the garden. Ideal transplant times vary from plant to plant, depending on the growing temperatures each prefers. In many cases, transplant times (often provided on seed packets) are given in terms of days before or after the last spring frost date for your area. See Set Up a Sowing Schedule on page 24 for information on determining this date.

Catalogs and local Extension offices provide calendars that indicate when flowers and vegetables can be safely transplanted outdoors. It is important to get local information on transplant times. If you search the Internet for transplanting recommendations, be sure that your source is located in the same area where you garden, and not in a much warmer or colder zone.

Also take into consideration the weather from the current growing season. In a wet, cold spring, the soil may be too wet and too cold for crops to go into the garden as scheduled, whether you're planting cold-tolerant cabbages or heat-loving peppers. Check the soil moisture before you transplant. Ask experienced gardening friends and neighbors when they are planning to transplant, or ask your local Cooperative Extension Service if you're unsure of whether it's time to transplant.

Prepare Soil before Transplanting

Getting the garden ready for transplants is just as important as preparing seedlings for the move and handling plants carefully during the transplanting process. Moving transplants into moist, prepared soil reduces the stress new transplants face, which helps them recover more quickly from transplanting.

When preparing soil and moving plants, try to avoid walking on the soil. If possible, work from a pathway. Another option is to put down a board and stand on that while you work to distribute your weight more evenly.

Loosen and amend soil. Whether you're planting garden rows filled with vegetable transplants or adding annuals here and there throughout the garden, loosen the soil to at least a shovel's depth. Work in plenty of organic matter before transplanting, and use a rake to create a smooth and level surface.

Check soil moisture. Test to see if your soil is too wet or too dry to dig. See Is the Soil Ready? on page 95 for details. If the soil is dry, water thoroughly a day before working the soil. Soil that's dry pulls moisture out of plant roots and damages them.

Pre-warm soil for heat-loving plants. Transplants that relish warm weather, including peppers and eggplants, are best planted into warm soil. In areas with long growing seasons, waiting to transplant until the soil warms up works just fine. If you want to get an early start, or if your growing season is short, you can give the soil a heat boost to help ease the transition to the garden. Two weeks or more before transplant time, prepare the soil and rake the site smooth. Water if soil is very dry. Spread black plastic over the site, stretching it tight and burying all the edges. Let the sun's rays warm the soil for 2 weeks before transplanting. Plant directly into the plastic by cutting holes through it with a trowel or gardening knife. The plastic holds heat during the nighttime hours, which also benefits heat-loving crops.

> ## Weed!
> *Tough, resilient weeds are your seedlings' worst enemies, so take steps to defeat them before you transplant. Dig up annuals and the roots of perennial weeds as you prepare soil. Mulch immediately after planting to keep weeds from coming back. A layer of newspaper, 6 to 8 sheets thick, under bark mulch will keep most weeds at bay. Keep mulch about 1 inch away from transplant stems to provide maximum air circulation and prevent disease problems.*

Getting Used to the Great Outdoors

Seedlings grown indoors are accustomed to pampered conditions. In order to succeed out in the garden, though, they need to be able to withstand sun, wind, and fluctuating temperatures. Sudden changes cause transplant shock and can check a plant's growth or even kill it. Hardening off is the process used to gradually prepare seedlings for life in the outside world.

"Easy does it" is the key to success. To begin the process, water plants thoroughly. Then look for a site that is shaded and protected from wind such as on the north side of a building or under a shrub or hedge. A screen porch may provide ideal

Ideal Transplanting Weather

An overcast, even drizzly day is ideal for transplanting because it minimizes stress to seedlings. If you have to transplant on a sunny day, protect plants once they're in the ground. Cover them with upside-down baskets propped on sticks to allow air circulation. Or create tents using burlap or row-cover fabric to provide shade while plants settle in.

conditions for hardening off. Move pots or flats outside to the protected spot and leave them out about an hour the first day. Over the course of a week, gradually increase the amount of time daily until plants remain outside all day and then all night long. During this process, also gradually expose plants to more sun and less protection from wind. If the weather turns cold, move plants back indoors each night. If slugs are a problem in your area, set pots up off the ground.

If you work away from home, start this process on a Friday afternoon, and increase the time and sun exposure over the weekend. On Monday, water plants and then set flats in a protected site before leaving them out during the day.

Harden off cold-tolerant plants first, including lettuce, cabbage, and broccoli along with hardy and half-hardy annuals. (See Easy Flowers Outdoors on page 110 for explanations of these terms.) Even these cold-tolerant plants can be damaged by frost or cold, wet weather, so watch the weather forecast and be prepared to protect plants (see Portable Protection on page 88) if there's a chance temperatures will dip too low.

Heat-lovers like peppers, eggplants, impatiens, and coleus are best moved to the garden only after nighttime temperatures remain above 60°F.

Another option is to move seedlings out into a cold frame or similar structure. Leave the cold frame sash open for longer periods each day. An unheated greenhouse or even plastic stretched over a simple frame can also be effective for hardening off seedlings. Open the end of the tunnel or the door of the greenhouse for a longer time each day. Water regularly and watch leaves carefully for signs of scorching. Keep an eye on the weather, and close up such structures when cold weather threatens.

TRANSPLANTING, STEP BY STEP

Earlier isn't necessarily better when it comes to moving seedlings outdoors, even if you're racing to produce the first tomatoes on your block. Exposure to weather that's too cold slows seedling growth rates. It can even affect performance all season long. Double-check planting dates before transplanting, either by checking seed packets or your sowing schedule, looking at seed catalogs, asking at local garden centers, or consulting your local Cooperative Extension Service.

In general, transplant most annuals and vegetables after the last spring frost date for your area. This is especially important for heat-loving seedlings such as tomatoes, eggplants, peppers, coleus, impatiens, and begonias, all of which are best moved after the soil has completely warmed up. Some plants such as cabbage, broccoli, violas, and pansies will tolerate a light frost and can go out several weeks before the last frost date.

See Spacing: Beds, Rows, or Broadcasting? on page 99 for options on garden planting patterns that maximize yield and help cut down on maintenance. Then move the plants as follows:

1. Do a moisture check. Soil in both pots and in the garden where you plan to transplant should be moist but not wet. Water deeply, if necessary.

2. Dig a planting hole. The hole should be a little bit bigger than the plant's rootball and about as deep.

3. Turn the plant out. With fingers on each side of the seedling, turn the pot upside down. Tap the bottom of the pot to ease the seedling out of its pot.

4. Set the transplant. Set transplants in their holes so they sit at about the same depth they were growing in the pot. The top of the rootball should be deep enough that it can be covered by about ¼ inch of soil. Fill in with soil around the rootball, then feather out the remaining loose soil so that it's smoothly distributed around the planting area.

5. Ensure good soil-to-root contact. Press the soil gently but firmly to ensure good contact between soil and roots.

6. Water well. Soak the soil immediately after planting to reduce transplant shock and to eliminate air pockets.

Portable Protection

Transplants often benefit from a bit of extra protection after they're moved to the garden, especially if the weather is unusually cold. If there's any chance that seedlings may be exposed to frost or extended cold (which can check their growth), use one of the options below to keep them snug and growing.

Leave the devices in place until plants recover from the shock of being transplanted. To determine if they have recovered, check to see that leaves are not wilted and plants have resumed growing. Don't hesitate to replace them if a cold snap occurs. These devices also are used to stretch the season by planting seedlings out earlier than normal to get an extra head start.

Hotcaps and cloches. Traditional cloches were bell-shaped plant covers made of glass, but today's models are more likely to be made of paper. Buy paper hot caps to cover seedlings, or make cloches out of a plastic milk bottle by cutting off the bottom. Unscrew the bottle cap to vent hot air during the day. Other devices are available from garden supply stores and catalogs, including water cloches, which are a type of cloche with walls constructed of plastic channels that you fill with water to offer extra insulation.

Row covers. These are transparent fabric sheets that can be used to cover a single plant or an entire row. They provide only a couple degrees of frost protection, but they do provide protection from wind and a bit of shade as well. Floating row covers also provide excellent control for a wide range of pests. Lay them loosely directly over the plants, or suspend them on hoops or bent stakes, and pile soil over the fabric edges all the way around. For extra frost protection, cover plants with two layers of row covers.

Plastic covers. Sheets of plastic can be used in a variety of ways to protect seedlings. Wrap them around cages or stakes to protect plants from wind. Or stretch them over hoops to cover an entire row, but be aware that you have to monitor the temperature under the plastic. Open the ends of the tunnel to provide ventilation.

Nursery Beds

Vegetables and annuals normally are transplanted right into the garden, but perennials and woody plants often need time to grow and get established before they are large enough to hold their own out in the real world. A nursery bed is a great spot for coddling small plants, and it's also perfect for pampering purchased plants that need some time and increased size before they are ready to be planted out.

You can also use a nursery bed to grow annuals so you have backup plants to move into an unexpected empty spot in the garden. Or sow hardy annuals like pot marigold (*Calendula officinalis*), larkspur (*Consolida ajacis*), and sweet alyssum (*Lobularia maritima*) outdoors in the nursery bed in fall, then the following spring transplant seedlings to where they are to bloom. A nursery bed is also handy for growing biennials for their first, non-blooming year. Foxglove (*Digitalis purpurea*) and Canterbury bells (*Campanula medium*) are two popular biennials. Grow them in a nursery bed the first year, then transplant them to the garden to bloom the second year. Here's how to build a great nursery bed:

Select a convenient site. Look for a spot that's close enough to where you garden that you can check on plants daily and keep a close eye on them. Easy access to a hose is important.

Consider exposure. Pick a spot that's protected from wind, if possible. While a full-sun site will work, partial shade is better to protect tiny plants from day-long baking sun. If you grow shade plants as well as sun-lovers, build a second nursery bed in a shady spot. If partial shade isn't available, consider using shade cloth suspended over hoops to protect plants. Shade cloth is available from garden supply stores and catalogs.

Prepare the soil. Dig the soil to at least a shovel's depth, work in plenty of organic matter, and rake it smooth.

Plant in blocks or rows. To make it easy to keep track of your various transplants, arrange plants in rows or blocks. That way they are easy to tend and can be transplanted easily.

CARE AFTER PLANTING

For a thriving, productive garden, keep a close eye on new transplants. Regular watering and extra protection from the elements will help them put down roots and get well established and growing strongly.

Provide sun protection. Especially if you were not able to transplant on a cloudy or rainy day, cover transplants with bushel baskets, old wicker baskets, large cardboard cartons, burlap propped over stakes, or other sun shades for a day or two. Prop up baskets, cartons, and other covers to provide air circulation.

Water, water, and more water. Water transplants before they are transplanted, as soon as they're in the ground, and then continue to water daily or every other day for about a week until the plants are well established and growing. After that, water them when you water the rest of your garden. Water perennials and woody plants weekly for the first year to encourage them to develop good, strong, deep roots.

Watering Wisdom

It pays to plan how you're going to water before you plant. In a vegetable garden, supplemental watering is essential. Soaker hoses make it easy to keep seedlings supplied with regular moisture. Install soaker hoses before you transplant, and set out transplants along the soaker hoses.

PART 3

SOWING SEEDS OUTDOORS

Sowing seeds directly in the garden where the plants are to grow is one of the most satisfying gardening activities. What could be simpler? Clear a patch of soil, rake it smooth, scatter seeds, and add water. Seedlings eventually appear, as if by magic. Of course, it can be a little more complicated than that, as gardeners have all sorts of tips and tricks they use to increase germination percentage, improve seedling performance, and get plants growing vigorously.

Direct sowing is the most common method for planting a wide variety of vegetables. It's also effective for planting many kinds of annuals and some perennials and woody plants. In this section you'll learn techniques for germinating a wide variety of plants right where they are to grow. In addition to the best methods for preparing soil so seedlings can thrive, you'll also learn spacing systems that increase production in the vegetable garden, and what crops and flowers are easiest from seeds.

GETTING YOUR GARDEN READY FOR SEEDS

SOME SEEDS SPROUT WHEN TOSSED onto soil that hasn't been prepared, but for a much better chance of success plan on preparing the soil before you sow. Start the preparation by having your soil tested to determine pH and to see if it's deficient in any of the major nutrients. Contact your local Cooperative Extension office, or see Resources and Links on page 115, for information on where to get a soil test.

Dig the soil to a shovel's depth, and spread a generous amount of organic matter such as compost or leaf mold over the site. If you're preparing soil for a vegetable garden, you may want to use a tiller to loosen and amend the soil. As you work, break up clumps of soil and remove rocks.

Dig or pull weeds and toss them aside instead of chopping them up. Toss fleshy rooted perennials into the trash. If not too weedy, chunks of sod can be added to compost; turn the chunks upside down and check regularly to make sure they don't resprout. As you dig or till, keep an eye out for the roots of perennial weeds like dandelions and grasses. Chopping weed roots into pieces essentially propagates them; you may end up with hundreds of smaller weeds, each of which grew from a tiny piece of chopped-up root. These will be much more vigorous than your tiny seedlings and can quickly overwhelm the desired plants.

If your soil test recommends it, apply a balanced organic fertilizer at the rate listed on the product label or the soil test recommendations. It is important not to overfertilize; read package directions and follow them carefully. Too much fertilizer causes rank, leafy growth at the expense of fruit and flowers, and it can make plants more susceptible to insect and diseases. Add amendments to adjust pH only if recommended by the soil test, and apply only the recommended amounts. Soil pH that is too alkaline or too acid will impair a plant's ability to take up nutrients.

SEEDBEDS 101.
To get the soil ready for seeds, rake it smooth after incorporating organic matter and any recommended amendments. Break up clods and remove any rocks or other debris.

After incorporating organic matter, rake the site smooth. If you aren't going to plant right away, it's a good idea to cover the soil with mulch to keep weeds at bay. Use compost, shredded bark, or other mulch. Spreading 6 to 8 sheets of newspaper under the mulch will keep weeds from sprouting. When you're ready to plant, just scrape the mulch aside and cut or poke a hole through the paper to get access to the soil.

Is the Soil Ready?

Digging soil that's too wet or too dry isn't good for it. Working very wet or dry soil destroys the soil structure, the beneficial crumbs and clumps that make up good soil. Good soil structure makes it easy for water and air to move through soil, and seedlings need both water and air elements to grow. Soil structure also determines how well roots can grow through soil. Digging soil when it is too dry breaks crumbs and clumps down into powder, leaving little room for air to move through the soil. Digging when the soil is too wet causes it to lump into hard, bricklike clods, also destroying structure.

To figure out if your soil is ready to dig, grab a handful and crush it in your palm, then press on it gently with a finger. If the soil crumbles apart easily into smaller chunks, it's ready to dig. If it won't form a clump when crushed or breaks apart into dust, it's too dry — water the site deeply and wait a day before testing again. If the soil in your hand forms a clod that won't break apart easily, it's probably too wet. Wait a day or two before preparing the soil.

Warm Up for Sowing

Prewarming soil isn't just for heat-loving transplants like peppers and eggplants. To get an early start on sowing seeds outdoors, spread black plastic mulch over the bed 2 weeks before it's time to sow. This warms soil and helps speed germination of even cold-loving crops like peas and cabbage.

It's a good idea to get in the habit of *always* adding organic matter every time you dig or till. Compost is an excellent source. Adding organic matter to soil adds nutrients, improves its ability to retain moisture, helps wet soil drain better, and improves soil structure. All these make soil better for the plants growing in your garden.

Is It Time to Sow?

If the soil is too cold, seeds tend to sit and rot rather than germinate. Use these tips to determine if you should sow now or wait for warmer weather.

Determine sowing dates. Mark the date of your last spring frost on your gardening calendar. (See Set Up a Sowing Schedule for how to determine frost dates, page 24.) Count backward to get dates for sowing cool-season crops and forward for warm-season ones. Consult the information on seed packets to determine how many days or weeks before or after frost that each type of seed can be sown. Keep in mind that these sowing dates are guidelines. Watch the weather and adjust sowing dates as necessary depending on the conditions in any particular year.

Check soil temperature. Using a compost or soil thermometer, test the soil temperature daily for 5 days, then add up all the readings and divide by 5 to determine the average soil temperature. Cool-season crops like peas, lettuce, and spinach, along with cool-weather annuals, germinate best when temperatures are between 45° and 60°F. Warm-season crops such as beans and corn, along with warm-weather annuals, germinate best when the soil is between 65° and 80°F.

Trust your experience. A great many gardeners judge soil temperature without using a thermometer. They dig up a handful of soil and estimate the temperature. Gardeners also determine sowing times by watching plants in their own yard and also by finding out what friends and gardening neighboring are planting. Corn seedlings growing in nearby fields are a sure sign that the soil is warm enough for warm-season crops.

PLANTING SEEDLINGS IN GEL

Getting seedlings growing extra early outdoors can be a fun challenge, and it's especially important in areas with short growing seasons, such as the Mountain West. Plant too early and the seeds rot because the soil is too cold. Using a gel to protect roots allows you to get an extra-early start, because seedlings of some plants can survive in soil that's too cold for the seeds to germinate. Use this technique for cold-tolerant plants such as lettuce, cabbage, beets, and carrots. First pregerminate seeds as described in Pregerminating on page 62. Then follow the steps below to suspend the new sprouts in a cornstarch gel, which protects them during the transplanting process. Here's how:

1. Make a gel using cornstarch, by boiling 1 tablespoon in a cup of water.

2. Cool the mixture completely, then scoop it into a small plastic bag.

3. Transfer the tiny sprouts to the gel. Very gently stir the sprouts in the gel, so they're not clumped together and won't all come out of the bag at once, then close the bag with a twist-tie.

4. To plant, dig a furrow or planting hole as you would if planting seeds.

5. Cut a corner off the bag and squeeze the seedlings out one at a time, gel and all, onto the soil. Sprinkle soil lightly over the seedlings. Water after planting, and water regularly as they become established. Install row covers over the bed to help protect seedlings from cold weather.

SPACING: BEDS, ROWS, OR BROADCASTING?

BEFORE YOU PLANT THAT FIRST SEED, figure out what pattern works best for your garden and for what you're growing. The traditional image of a vegetable garden has long been a rectangular space with crops planted in straight rows. While traditional rows work just fine for sowing seeds and raising vegetables, creating planting beds allows you to grow more vegetables in less space. Sometimes called intensive or wide-row beds, these allow you to grow crops closer together, with less space devoted to unplanted work areas between rows. Edible flowers and flowers for cutting or drying can also be sown in beds. For more ideas on planting arrangements for annuals or other flowers, see Sowing in the Flower Garden on page 109.

Planting Bed Basics

In order to succeed with planting beds, you need soil amended with plenty of compost and other organic matter to support more plants in less space. Such soil provides perfect conditions for sowing seeds directly in the garden — and for transplants. Here's what you need to know:

- Beds can be level with the surrounding soil or they can be raised, with the soil surface several inches above the surrounding area. In areas where rainfall is at a premium, consider creating beds that are lower than the surrounding area to collect every drop of rainfall.

- Raised beds are a good idea because they provide improved soil and ideal drainage. Also, closer plant spacing means you can grow more plants in less space. Closer spacing also leaves less room for weeds. The sides of raised beds can be framed with wood, or the soil can be simply raked up to form a long mound.

- Make each bed narrow enough that you can easily reach the center from the sides, from 3 to perhaps 5 feet wide depending on your reach. That way, you can tend plants without stepping on the soil. It's best to create beds that aren't too long, as well. Otherwise it's tempting to cut across beds if you need to move from one row to another. Walking on soil compacts it, making it less suitable for growing plants.

BED BORDERS. Raised beds can be framed by boards, landscape ties, or block walls. Or, create them by simply raking soil up into a mound (facing page).

- Plant the entire surface of the bed to take advantage of the rich soil. Seed packets often list spacing requirements for wide rows as well as traditional single rows. Broadcast seeds evenly across the entire bed. Once they sprout, thin to leave the recommended space between each plant.

- Mulch plants, and keep any unplanted soil covered with mulch to prevent weeds, conserve moisture, and moderate changes to soil temperature.

- Beds for wide-row planting can be any shape you like, although rectangular is traditional. Arrange several together to make an otherwise traditional-looking vegetable garden, or tuck them in here and there throughout your landscape.

- Plant in beds by broadcasting seed in bands, planting in blocks, or by arranging several rows of seeds or transplants close together. Leave space between these wide rows so you can get in to weed and tend plants.

Traditional Rows

Straight rows with paths running in between make it simple and straightforward to lay out the garden. It's a very practical system if you use a tiller or tractor to prepare the soil. For small gardens, however, it isn't the most space-efficient system, since pathways take up several feet on each side of each row. Where space is limited, you're better off planting wide rows in beds.

Broadcasting

To sow seed over a large area — for example, sowing grass seed for a lawn or wildflower seed for a meadow — you need a different strategy from traditional rows or wide beds. Rake the soil smooth and scatter seeds thinly across the whole area. Then rake the soil gently in the opposite direction to cover the seed. Water with a gentle stream of water from a hose or watering can. This method is called broadcasting. You can also use broadcasting for sowing leaf lettuce mixes, mesclun, and other cut-and-come-again crops in wide beds.

How Deep?

Check seed packets for recommendations on how deep seeds need to be planted. Vegetables like corn and beans are planted about 1 inch deep, peas from ¾ to 1 inch, while beets are planted about ½ inch deep. If you don't have a specific recommendation, use the width of the seed as a guideline: sow at a depth equal to the width.

Raise 'em Up!

Melons, pumpkins, and winter squash benefit from being sown in 1-foot-tall, 2- to 3-foot-wide mounds or hills made of rich, loose soil mixed with compost. The hills or mounds of soil heat up more quickly than the surrounding soil, which is helpful for these crops, and adding a generous amount of compost or other organic matter will help hold moisture in the soil, as well. For extra-rich hills, dig holes 1 foot deep and 1 foot wide under each spot where you're planning on building a hill. Fill the hole with compost or well-rotted manure, then build up a hill of soil and compost on top of the site. Your plants will appreciate this extra dose of organic matter once their roots reach down into this special cache.

PLANTING MOUNDS. For perfect drainage and fertility, provide vigorous, vining crops with rich, loose mounds of soil mixed with compost.

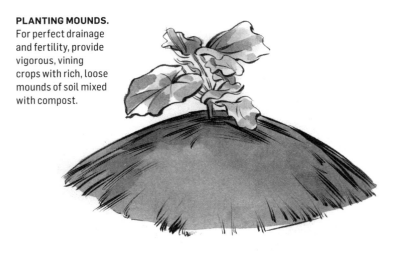

SOWING SEEDS, STEP BY STEP

Once the soil is prepared and raked smooth, it's time to sow. To avoid compacting the soil, either work from the paths between beds or rows, or place a board on the soil and stand on the board to distribute your weight. Here's how to sow your seeds:

1. If you are planting traditional straight rows, stretch a string between stakes placed at either end of the row. Instead of string, you can mark the row with a dusting of horticultural lime (the rock powder used to adjust soil pH; widely available at garden centers) or with the corner of a hoe.

    For wide rows in planting beds, mark off blocks or multiple rows the same way.

2. Of course, plants don't care if your rows are straight. Feel free to get creative. Depending on the site and the style of your garden, curving rows may be more suitable. Mark curves with a stick, a dusting of lime, or the corner of a hoe.

3. Make a shallow furrow with the corner of hoe following the desired planting line or curve. To make a wider planting area for wide beds, use the flat side of a hoe. A trowel or gardening knife works well for short furrows.

4. Space out the seeds along the row or across the bed according to packet directions. Take pinches of seed and sprinkle them thinly and evenly, or use a hand-held seed sower (see Handy Helpers, page 48). For mechanical seeders for large gardens, see Tools of the Trade, page 106. One option for sowing very fine seed is to mix it with  white play sand. That way, it's easy to see where you've already spread seeds. Sowing carefully, and thinly, helps minimize the need to thin seedlings later on.

5. Use a rake or hoe to gently cover the seeds. Then water, using a fine mist to avoid dislodging the seeds.

6. To prevent birds, rabbits, and other pests from gobbling up newly sown seed or seedlings, cover seedbeds after planting with wire mesh folded at the corners to form a box. Or install row covers over beds. Row covers also help keep insect pests at bay and provide a couple degrees of frost protection. Remove them when plants begin to flower, so insects can pollinate crops.

7. Water daily (if there is no rain) to keep the seedbed evenly moist, but not wet, while seedlings germinate and become established.

Tools of the Trade

While conventional tools are fine for planting small spaces, if you're planting a large garden, consider some of the following:

Hand-held tools for wide beds. Extra-wide rakes designed to handle raised beds and wide rows are available. Traditional hoes are about 5 inches wide; collinear hoes with blades as wide as 7 inches are ideal for preparing wide beds or managing weeds in garden pathways.

Broadcast spreader or seeder. Broadcast spreaders dispense seeds from a hopper and are ideal for spreading grass seed or cover crop seed evenly over a large area. They can also be used to spread many types of fertilizer and limestone evenly over a lawn or a large garden.

Mechanical seeders. These are precision tools designed to roll over the garden and spread seed evenly along rows or across a predetermined area. For large gardens they save a lot of time. Look for ones that can be adjusted to handle a variety of seed sizes; usually there are interchangeable plates for different sizes of seed. Also look for models that will dig a furrow and cover it up, and that let you adjust the depth of the furrow for different types of seeds.

Easy Vegetables to Direct-Sow

The crops below are best sown directly in the garden where they are to grow. Crops marked with an asterisk (*) need soil that is at least 60°F. Unmarked crops prefer cool weather and are best sown when the soil is at least 45°F. Most of these cool-season crops can be sown in both spring and fall.

- Arugula
- Asian greens (mizuna, pak choi, mustard greens)
- Beans (snap, bush, pole) *
- Beans, fava
- Beans, lima (sow once soil is above 75°F)
- Beets
- Carrots
- Corn salad, mâche
- Cucumbers (sow once soil is above 70°F)
- Lettuce and lettuce mixes
- Melons (sow once soil is above 70°F)
- Mesclun
- Okra (sow once soil is above 70°F)
- Onions
- Peas (snap, snow, shelling)
- Radishes (best sown when soil is above 50°F)
- Soybeans, edamame (sow once soil is above 50°F)
- Spinach (best sown when soil is above 50°F)
- Squash, zucchini (sow once soil is above 70°F)
- Sweet corn, popcorn *
- Swiss chard
- Winter squash, gourd, and pumpkin (sow once soil is above 70°F)

Spacing 101

Taking time to space seeds properly reduces the essential chore later on of thinning seedlings. Crowded seeds or seedlings compete with one another for light and nutrients, and the result is less-vigorous plants with lower yields or fewer flowers. Tearing off the corner of a seed packet and sprinkling seed on a prepared site is an easy way to sow, but you'll get better results if you use one of the methods below to space seeds:

- Measure spacing with a trowel or gardening knife, many of which are marked for this purpose.

- Mark lengths on a slender, lightweight board about 2 feet long, or cut notches to make a handy spacer that you can place along a row. Mark off or cut notches every 3 inches.

- For large gardens, consider using a mechanical seeder, which disperses large amounts of seeds evenly from a hopper. See Tools of the Trade on page 106.

- Consider spacing out seeds at your kitchen table *before* you go out in the garden by making your own seed tapes. See Do-It-Yourself Seed Tapes, page 18, for directions.

Install Supports before You Plant

Pole beans, tall varieties of peas, and morning glories need a trellis or other support to grow on. If you are growing these or other plants that need support, it's best to install posts or trellises before you sow seed to avoid damaging plant roots or stems.

SOWING IN THE FLOWER GARDEN

MANY ANNUALS ARE PERFECTLY HAPPY being sown outdoors in the garden right where they are to grow and bloom. They can be grown in traditional rows or wide rows in beds exactly like vegetables. To grow flowers for cutting or drying, raised beds and rows make perfect sense. Much more often, though, flowers are sown in drifts or patches in garden beds and borders.

EASY FLOWERS OUTDOORS. When direct-sowing flowers out in the garden, rake sections of soil smooth, sow seeds, and then gently cover the seeds with soil. Water regularly until seedlings are well established.

Easy Flowers Outdoors

In addition to classifying annuals as cool- or warm-season, gardeners also use the terms hardy, half-hardy, or tender. These terms give a hint as to when the seeds are best sown and grown.

Hardy annuals (H) tolerate light frost or freezing weather. They are sown outdoors in fall for germination the following spring, or as soon as the soil can be worked in late winter or early spring.

Half-hardy annuals (HH) withstand cold, damp weather but not frost. They are typically sown outdoors on or around the last spring frost date.

Tender annuals (T) need warm soil for best germination. Wait to sow them outdoors until the soil temperature is above 60°F. Generally, that means 2 or 3 weeks after the last spring frost date in your area. A soil thermometer will give you precise information, which is a good idea if weather has been unseasonably cold.

The following annuals need no special treatment, so you can just sow them outdoors where they are to grow. Use the letter(s) after each plant name below to determine when to plant, according to the terms defined above.

- Amaranth, love-lies-bleeding (*Amaranthus caudatus*) T
- Bachelor's button (*Centaurea cyanus*) H
- Bells-of-Ireland (*Moluccella laevis*) HH
- Calendula, pot marigold (*Calendula officinalis*) HH

- California poppy (*Eschscholzia californica*) H
- Candytuft (*Iberis umbellata*) H
- Celosia, cockscomb (*Celosia argentea*) T
- Cleome, spider flower (*Cleome hassleriana*) HH
- Corn poppy (*Papaver rhoeas*) H
- Cosmos (*Cosmos* species) T
- Hyacinth bean (*Lablab purpureus*) T
- Larkspur (*Consolida ajacis*) H
- Lavatera, tree mallow (*Lavatera trimestris*) H
- Mexican sunflower (*Tithonia rotundifolia*) T
- Morning glories (*Ipomoea* species) T
- Nasturtium (*Tropaeolum majus*) T
- Nigella, love-in-a-mist (*Nigella damascena*) HH
- Scarlet runner bean (*Phaseolus coccineus*) T
- Sunflower (*Helianthus annuus*) T
- Sweet pea (*Lathyrus odoratus*) H
- Zinnias (*Zinnia* species) T

For planting a garden of all annuals, or adding patches of flowers among perennials, first identify the area to be sown. Mark the area to be sown by drawing a line around it with a stick, marking it off with stakes and string, adding a small flag — whatever works for you. Loosen the soil and work in some compost or other organic matter, then rake it smooth. Either broadcast seeds over the entire area or place them individually, arranging in free-form rows or just spaced at random. Be sure to add a label to keep track of what flowers are planted where. A marker also serves as a valuable reminder that the spot needs regular watering until the seeds are up and the plants are well established.

Sow Them Once

"Self-sowing" annuals are ones that produce and scatter seeds that germinate in subsequent years. Hardy annuals are the most common self-sowers, but many different annuals will sow themselves in the garden.

CARING FOR SEEDS AND SEEDLINGS

While it's lovely to think about scattering flower seed and just waiting for flowers to appear, a *laissez-faire* approach rarely brings good results. To give your newly sown flowers a good start in life — and to ensure beautiful flowers later in the season — use these steps to get plants off to a robust start.

Watering. In early spring, the soil is often moist and cool enough that you often don't need to water regularly. Seeds won't sprout in dry soil, though, so keep a close eye on soil moisture. Water during dry spells or when the weather gets unusually warm, at least until seedlings are up and have produced two or more sets of true leaves. For summer sowings, or in areas where spring weather tends to be warm, water daily. Always water with a fine mist to avoid washing away the seeds or seedlings; use a hose attachment specifically designed to supply a gentle mist. If the weather is hot and dry, try covering the seedbed with burlap or row covers. These coverings help keep the soil moist and cool. Check daily for seedlings and remove the covering as soon as you see signs of sprouting.

Weeding. The first plants you see are likely to be weeds. To keep these rugged plants from stealing nutrients and shading out desired plants, it's important to weed early and often. If you aren't sure just what is a weed and what is a seedling, Resources and Links on page 115 includes websites that feature photographs of common weeds and seedling plants so you can tell which is which. Use a hoe or hand-held weeder to dispatch weeds growing in the row. For ones that appear near where seedlings are sown, it's safest to clip them off at ground level using scissors. This minimizes damage to surrounding seedlings.

Thinning. This is a task that many gardeners dislike, because it involves cutting off or pulling perfectly healthy seedlings. Proper spacing is vital for healthy growth, though, so thinning seedlings is an essential task.

Once seedlings have two or more sets of true leaves and are growing vigorously, check the final spacing recommendations on the seed packets or in your notes. You can thin once or you can do it in stages, removing a few seedlings in several different sessions until plants are growing at their final spacing. To thin, clip off extra seedlings at the ground level with scissors. If you're careful, you can also pull up extra seedlings. Water the soil before pulling plants, then put your fingers on either side of the seedling to be removed in order to steady the ground around it and avoid damaging remaining seedlings.

Mulching. Once plants are at their final spacing, mulch the rows to prevent weeds from sprouting and to keep the soil moist. Use compost, shredded leaves, shredded bark, or other mulch. You can spread up to 6 or 8 sheets of newspaper under the mulch to make a stronger weed barrier.

INDEX

RESOURCES AND LINKS

Cooperative Extension offices. To find your local office, look in the telephone directory under city or county government. To find the website on the Internet, search for "Cooperative Extension Service" and the name of your state, or visit:
   www.csrees.usda.gov/Extension

Specific germination requirements. Gardeners who plant perennials from seed and need additional germination information will want to bookmark Tom Clothier's Garden Walk and Talk page. He has extensive databases with germination requirements for perennials (including a separate database for *Penstemon* species), annuals, trees, and shrubs.
   http://tomclothier.hort.net

The Backyard Gardener page has a Seed Germination Database of germination requirements. The information at this site is supplied by Thompson & Morgan, a huge seed company.
   www.backyardgardener.com/tm.html

Seedling and weed photos. If you're weeding and are trying to determine which seedlings are crops and which are weeds, it helps to see photos of what you're trying to grow. Photographs of vegetable and herb seedlings from artichoke to squash are available at The Westside Gardener's Vegetable and Herb Seedling Photographs page:

http://westsidegardener.com/guides/seedlings

The Weed Science Society of America also has a good website. It provides photographs of weeds and native wild plants at various stages of growth:

www.wssa.net

The Seed Site has pictures of seedpods, seeds, and seedlings. It also offers information on germination requirements:

http://theseedsite.co.uk

Seed information for teachers. The SeedImages.com site, run by Colorado State University, features links to various sites on seed identification, dormancy, and much more:

www.seedimages.com/SeedResources.aspx

Seed saving. A useful book is *Seed Sowing and Saving* by Carole B. Turner (Storey Publishing, 1998); it contains information on collecting, cleaning, and saving seeds. Online, start by looking at the information on preserving heirloom seeds on the Seed Savers Exchange website, *www.seedsavers.org*. Their book *Seed to Seed*, by Suzanne Ashworth, contains extensive information on saving seeds.

Soil tests. To find a laboratory to test your soil, Cooperative Extension Service office, or search keywords "Soil Testing Labs" and the name of y

A soil test from a private lab usually costs r tional tests and more recommendations. For the mendations, choose a lab located in your region. run by University of Illinois Extension features a

http://urbanext.illinois.edu/soiltest

R

raised beds, 10, *10*, 100, *100*
record keeping, 17
row covers, 89

S

saving seeds. *See* storing seeds
scarification of seeds, 58
schedule for sowing, 24–29, 96–97
seed companies, local, 19
seeders, 106, 108
seed exchanges, 1
seedling(s). *See also* transplanting
    air circulation for, 68–69
    caring for, 113–14
    fertilizer for, 69–70
    held by leaf, not stem, 73
    instead of seed packets, 16–17
    pests and, 30–31
    planting in gel, 97–98, *98*
    pots for fussy, 42
    potting mixes for, 39
    rotten at soil line, 30, *30*
    thinning, 65, *65*
    transplant times, 26–27
seed packets
    information on, 12–13, 25
    quantity of, 16–17
seed(s). *See also* storing seeds
    caring for, 113–14
    catalog information, 12–13
    depth for planting, 102
    magic of, 1–4
    reasons to plant, 2–4
    shapes and sizes, 13, *13*
    treated/untreated, 15
seed sowers or handlers, 49, *49*

seed starters, self-watering, 41, *41*
seed starting. *See* sowing seeds
        indoors; sowing seeds outdoors
seed-starting mixes, 37, 39, 56
seed tapes, *18*, 18–19
self-pollinated plants, 32
shade, 9, 11, 90
shrubs from seed, 77
site selection, 10, *10*, 11, 90
soil. *See also* mixes
    amendments, 94
    compaction, 100
    depth for seeds, 102
    digging, readiness for, 95–96
    moisture, transplanting, 81, 85
    "pots" from, *45*, 45–47, *46*, *47*
    preparation, transplanting, 80–82
    prewarming, 95
    for seedbeds, 94, *94*
    temperature, 96
    testing, 11, 117
soil blocks, 45–47, *46*, *47*
sorting seeds, 26, *26*, 27
sowing seeds indoors. *See*
        also containers
    annuals, easy, 57
    density of seeds, 52, *52*
    and germinating outdoors, 76–77
    lights for, 50–51, *51*
    mixes and, 37, 39, 53
    pressure on medium, 56
    seed starters, self-watering, 41, *41*
    step by step, 53–56, *54*, *55*, *56*
    tools for, 35–36, 48–49
    vegetables, easy, 55
    work area for, 36
sowing seeds outdoors. *See also*
        garden; spacing; weather

in batches, 28, *28*
experiments with, 28
flower garden, *109*, 109–12
one by one, 49, *49*
plant types and, 92
scheduling for, 24–29, 96–97
seed sorting for, 26, *26*, 27
step by step, 104–5, *105*
transplant times and, 26–27
spacing, 99–108
basics, 108
broadcasting, 102, 106
planting bed basics,
99–101, *100*, *101*
planting mounds, 103, *103*
rows, traditional, 102
seed tapes and, *18*, 18–19
special-needs seeds, 58–63
storing seeds, 9, 32–34, *34*
stratification, 59–61, *60*
sun/sunlight
hours per day, 11
for nursery beds, 90
windowsills and, 50
supports/posts/trellises, 108

T

temperature, 64, 66
tender annuals, 110
thinning, 65, *65*, 114
tools
garden, 49, 106
indoor seed starting, 35–36, 48–49
transplanting. *See also* seedling(s)
covers/protection, 88–89, 91
hardening off, 82–84
into nursery beds, 89–90
soil moisture, 81, 85

soil preparation, 80–82
step by step, 84–88, *85*, *86*, *87*, *88*
weeds and, 82
trees from seed, 77

V

vegetables. *See also* crops
cool-weather, 7–8, 27, 97, 107
to direct sow, 107
heat-loving, 8, 27
planting mounds for, 103
for shade, 9
starting indoors, 55
vining crops, 77, 103, 108

W

watering, 113
automatic, 41, *41*
even moisture, 66, 68
transplants, 91
weather
frost dates, 25
transplants and, 83
weeds/weeding, 82, 93, 113–14, 115
wide-row beds, 99, 101

OTHER STOREY TITLES YOU WILL ENJOY

The Complete Guide to Saving Seeds, **by Robert Gough
& Cheryl Moore-Gough.**
A comprehensive guide to collecting, saving, and cultivating the
seeds of more than 300 vegetables, herbs, and more.
320 pages. Paper. ISBN 978-1-60342-574-2.

The Dirt-Cheap Green Thumb, **by Rhonda Massingham Hart.**
Tips and tricks to help pennywise gardeners preserve their budgets.
288 pages. Paper. ISBN 978-1-60342-441-7.

Saving Seeds, **by Marc Rogers.**
Plant-by-plant advice on how to select, raise, harvest, and store
seeds for more than 100 vegetables and flowers commonly grown
in home gardens.
192 pages. Paper. ISBN 978-0-88266-634-1.

Secrets of Plant Propagation, **by Lewis Hill.**
Expert advice on techniques to grow beautiful, bountiful, healthy
plants — and save money in the process!
176 pages. Paper. ISBN 978-0-88266-370-8.

The Vegetable Gardener's Bible, 2nd edition, **by Edward C. Smith.**
The 10th Anniversary Edition of the vegetable gardening classic, with
expanded coverage and additional vegetables, fruits, and herbs.
352 pages. Paper. ISBN 978-1-60342-475-2. Hardcover. ISBN 978-1-60342-476-9.

The Year-Round Vegetable Gardener, **by Niki Jabbour.**
How to grow your own food 365 days a year, no matter where you live!
256 pages. Paper. ISBN 978-1-60342-568-1. Hardcover. ISBN 978-1-60342-992-4.

These and other books from Storey Publishing are available
wherever quality books are sold or by calling 1-800-441-5700.
Visit us at *www.storey.com*.